Primary Love

The Elemental Nature of Human Love, Intimacy, and Attachment

Randall S. Klein

UNIVERSITY PRESS OF AMERICA, ® INC.
Lanham • Boulder • New York • Toronto • Plymouth, UK

Copyright © 2010 by
University Press of America,® Inc.
4501 Forbes Boulevard
Suite 200
Lanham, Maryland 20706
UPA Acquisitions Department (301) 459-3366

Estover Road
Plymouth PL6 7PY
United Kingdom

Library of Congress Control Number: 2010922748
ISBN: 978-0-7618-5111-0 (paperback : alk. paper)
eISBN: 978-0-7618-5112-7

∞™ The paper used in this publication meets the minimum
requirements of American National Standard for Information
Sciences—Permanence of Paper for Printed Library Materials,
ANSI Z39.48-1992

To my mother, Amy
—my primary love

Contents

Preface

In my twenty-five years of the clinical practice of psychotherapy I have been entranced by the uniquely human concept of love in all its resplendent forms and manifestations. As I listen attentively to my patients with fascination, I hear rather poignant and sometimes poetic descriptions of the experiences of being in love, falling in and out of love, painfully losing a beloved through death, and with fortunately less frequency, though the most tragic of all—a feeling of having never been in love. Yet, the concept of love has puzzled me. I have heard the testimonies of many persons who have experienced love in their lives, and these declarations have compelled me to fashion an intelligible and hopefully inspirational definition of it. However, it is this attempt I compare to viewing into a kaleidoscope. The variegated, changing patterns and scenes of love inspire me with awe, yet disillusion me. Inasmuch as my effort to define love has been futile, I realize that my quest has been no more than simply misdirected. In proper redirection, I present a rather simple and concise composition on love, intimacy, and attachment in their multiple descriptions and demonstrations, and in their uniquely human conceptualization. Should you desire a definition of love, I humbly refer you to the nearest dictionary.

There are many types of love in varying contexts: Love for a friend, a family member, or the love for a lover. There is a love for fellow mankind, a love for God, and a love for the beauty of the earth and universe. One may have a love for life. However, it is the thrust of my thesis to address love as the very driving force that cultivates and constructs the human personality. Love is the sine qua non of normal human psychological and social development. We will trace the evolution of love from the birth of the human infant to the mature love and intimacy of adulthood. This is, admittedly, far from a comprehensive and exhaustive study of the concept of love, nonetheless its line of thought tracks the heart of human interaction in the most intimate of experience and expression.

Love, intimacy, and attachment progressively transform, unfold, and expand in the contexts of intricate, interpersonal relationships through a person's lifespan. Human interaction becomes increasingly sophisticated as each individual proceeds through the sequential psychosocial stages of life, such as toddlerhood, childhood, adolescence, and young adulthood. With the transition into each new phase, however, the quality and nature of love does not deviate and alter from its quality and nature in preceding phases. Rather, love and intimacy, like all characteristics of human development, as they advance to a higher order of organization and manifestation, remain nonetheless founded on and secured in their primordial state—the attachment of an infant to its mother. The origin of love is found in that which transpires between a mother and her newborn baby. An individual's sense of love and intimacy develops in his or her own evolution, and yet he or she maintains the foundation of this sense through his or her life. The primacy of love is never relinquished as one ages and matures; it simply transmutes.

This book is a discussion of the psychoanalytic theory of the human emotion, the human experience, of love. As personal and subjective as the concept of love is, it is identified as an interpersonal experience, a relational phenomenon in which its constituent components of intimacy and attachment behavior are manifested necessarily within the context of relationships. Interpersonal psychologists suggest that love should not and dare not be investigated, either empirically or aesthetically, separate from social connection, from human development and maturation, and from the totality of the human self and its existence. This author concurs and further suggests that the study of a person's being is a study of its experience of love in either health and function or ill-health and dysfunction.

In the course of this study, love is investigated within the realm of its healthy acquisition, maintenance, and progression. Intimacy and attachment are explored in all of love's glory and splendor and personal enhancement. From this constructional viewpoint, it is to be clearly acknowledged and identified, however sadly, that love can and does fail in its normative process, falling prey to disarray, misguidance, and outright defect. This however, is to be the focus of another investigative pursuit. The focus of this study centers on nature's typical course of love, a relatively healthy love.

From the 1930's through the 1960's, a British psychoanalyst named Michael Balint diverged from a classical psychoanalytic thought and viewed love not as an integral component of the sexual instinct of purely biological origin, but theorized that love is an experience of a unique, yet universally human, relationship between the entirety of the self and another person. The healthy human being is born naturally embedded in social relatedness to other human beings and in the ideal, remains so embedded. At the beginning of life in the context of the mother-infant bond, the genesis of the phenomena of love, intimacy, and attachment, so conceived by Balint, is that the baby is, at and from the beginning, emotionally related to the mothering person. There is a primary and elemental sociality inherent in this relationship as the infant-child melds emotionally and perceptually with the mother who ministers to her baby's needs and wishes. This primitive, yet experientially potent, relationship is based on an implicit contract between the infant and its mother promising that her progeny's every physical and psychological need will be unqualifiedly and unquestionably met. An emotional communication is innate between infant and mother. To this fundamentally social experience, founded on immediate attachment and intimation, Michael Balint ascribed the term "primary love."[1]

At birth, the human infant instinctively reaches out for its mother and activates a mutual cueing and response system between itself and her. The newborn is geared socially to organize its own primitive, archaic experience toward a lovingly ministering environment that is there, perceivably, to unconditionally attend its needs. From birth, the infant does not passively receive the mother's care, rather the pliable yet fundamentally organized infant actively strives for these provisions. Reflex phenomena such as smiling, gazing, grasping, clinging, and sucking are primitively yet effectively conveyable skills for social engagement with the gratifying mother.

Attachment behavior on the part of the infant involves a necessary counterpart in the role of the mothering figure. The mothering instinct essentially fills this role. Mothering behavior may lie dormant until parenthood when it is primed and activated, processing along lines unique to the particular mother-infant bond. In this regard, maternal instinct is biologically predetermined, yet its expression will be dictated by the relationship between the mother and her baby. Primary love is a sociality based on mutuality and functional interdependence. Reaching outward for emotional connection inaugurates the capacity to love as well as to receive love. Being psychologically cared for, in all of its sensed goodness, is the stuff from which love is born.

The presence and the potency of primary love never cease. Love remains at the essential and elemental core of human existence, replayed and reorganized around specific biological, psychological, and social needs of the individual as he or she traverses the developmental and maturational course of life. Humans' relatively long period of dependence on parental support, nurture, and protection assures that one's love for the parents is an ongoing process. As life is an ongoing experience, so too, is love. Life and love are synonymous in human encounter. These two phenomena are mutually inclusive, each serving as context and aliment to the cultivation of the other.

We will investigate both the personal and interpersonal dynamics involved in the evolution and promulgation of love and intimacy that create the very essence of personhood through childhood, adolescence, and into adulthood. Of particular note will be the intricate connection between the experiences of love in adulthood and in early childhood. In fact, the encounter of mature love, intimacy, and attachment of adulthood is a recapitulation of the love that flows reciprocally between mother and infant. This is an adult love that in effect regresses to an infantile state in the service of both selves of the lovers. They recapture, yet transform, their primary experiences in effort to establish a relational configuration conducive to the functional interdependence of two mature, healthy adults. People never lose the original love of their lives, and their love forever has its origin in the tranquil, harmonious, and blissful, primal state of being psychologically held and contained in infancy by the wondrously good mother. The love of origin is a love that never dies.

Introduction:
This Thing We Call Love

"It's a beautiful necessity
of our nature
to love something."

—Douglas Jerrold
Early 19th century British reform writer

This particular quote I find impressive because of its inviting simplicity, a tru-ism which perhaps very few would care to renounce and perhaps equally few would care to ponder. Humans are inclined to take love for granted however personally significant and intense it may be. But what is this thing we call love? Most contemporary psychoanalysts believe that love is an emotion of great potency and potential, and it touches almost every person's life in vari-ous degrees and forms. Philosophers through the centuries have made admi-rable attempts to characterize the phenomenon of love only to capture its es-sence in crude yet tenable clichéd and proverbial form, as we have all heard: "Love is bliss;" "love is blind;" "love is forever;" is that which "makes the world go 'round." To many ancient Greek philosophers, love identifies the unquestionable supremacy of the powers of the gods. Mortals heralded love as a gift from the gods that offers the illusion of redemption and preservation so tenaciously clung to in face of the world's reality of complexity, dissen-tion, and oftentimes unattainable gratification. Love has often been spoken of with sanctity as something to be revered rather than studied. Moreover, love's presence is to be a miracle, it's absence a tragedy.

Yet, this gift from the gods was and still is approached tenuously, for many believe the phenomenon of love to be an inevitably destructive force, spoken of in metaphysical terms: "Love is madness, an insanity;" "love is child-ishness, a regressive force;" "love is disintegration, a melting away." This

1

duality is thought of by many as the quintessence of human ambivalence. Playwright William Shakespeare wrote of love as an amalgamation of bit-ter-sweet tastings both abhorred and desired, dreaded and glorified. Perhaps people necessarily experience love with great anxiety.

For those who insist on love's grandeur, it can enhance the very essence of nature and allow people to thrive. It can allow them to expand their relation to and recognition of all of nature's beauty—the sky, the ocean, the mountains, the trees, and all of the creatures of this earth, and encompass all things past, present, and future. Furthermore, love is perhaps the desire for all of life's beauty, a sense of oneness with the earth. I believe that not only serving to maintain our sanity, love is the very source of our capacity to exist, the very essence of our personhood. Without love, one fragments. Yet, people take great precaution not to transgress love, for fear that need, desire, and plea-sure might transmute into pain and dissolution. One wonders if the people of ancient Greece, as well as of today, see love as a virtue, a morality beyond conceptualization—a conscription to which to undenyingly adhere, yet not on which to perseverate for fear of overexertion towards an ideal of perfection and exaltation beyond one's reach. May I suggest that we take love, acknowl-edge it, experience it, and appreciate it for its powers, but do not question it.

With the exception of a few great thinkers, particularly those of ancient Greece such as Democritus, Empedocles, Parmenides, Plato, and Aristotle, the people of their times did not question the epistemology of human love. Yet, love was a part of their lives that they did not renounce. Democritus viewed love as the motivating link between man and all things beautiful that surrounded him. Empedocles considered Aphrodite, the Greek goddess of love, to be the very essence, in fact, the embodiment of every man, and the gentle guiding force of each person's benevolent thoughts and deeds. Similarly, Parmenides thought of love as the very thrust of all man's struggle for self-actualization. Plato believed Eros, the Greek god of love and desire, to be uniquely attached to man's knowledge and talents. Any person who is caressed by Eros with love is imbued with the virtues of music, song, poetry, art, knowledge, and wisdom. Aristotle conceptualized love in terms of kin-ship, and in particular, friendship, not only with another but also with one's self. Yet, love for another and love for oneself are intertwined. Love, accord-ing to Aristotle, is so consuming that it could be devoted at any given time to only one relationship between oneself and the beloved as an all encompassing attachment.

The inquisitions of contemporary man remain within the stream of thought of these early thinkers. However, as aforementioned, love remains a concept yet to be defined. Yet, most would agree that in some enigmatic way love is integrated into every aspect of human development. Love and human growth evolve in mutual influence. One might say that love is the very essence of human development.

Love is unquestionably a universal phenomenon and one that has beckoned some scientific inquiry within the last century. Because the human brain has developed substantially more in sophistication than of all other creatures, humans have been endowed with the capacity to experience love. Through modern science, love is understood as a life impulse, innate in mankind, and is originated from and manifested by a combination of biological and psychological forces. However, it is my view that the ability to love and be loved is perhaps the highest maturational achievement of man, and is more than a mere manifestation of the biological need to procreate. The act of coitus is to a much lesser extent guided by hormonal factors than by neural factors. The psychological components of love meet with the biological elements in comprising the energy force which psychoanalysis refers to as libido. It is libidinal energy, a combination of the early psychological components mentioned in the preface and those innate biochemical forces that encourage both personality formation and the manifestation of human beings' capacity to love. While this is indeed an oversimplified means of describing the phenomenon of love, it does, nonetheless, clear the path for investigation into its psychological and social aspects.

Sigmund Freud, the forerunner of the psychoanalytic movement at the close of the nineteenth century, assumed the arduous task of investigating the mental factors involved in the human personality, including sexuality and libido. To Freud, libido was not simply an instinct of biological origin innate in humans for specifically procreative function, but an inherently humanistic quality of the relationship of the self to another. Freud's conceptualization of libido was to a degree influenced by the writings of Greek mythologists and philosophers. Libido is much more than the manifest instinctual urge toward the person of one's gratifying source, leading ultimately to the capacity for copulation at the onset of puberty. As Eros was described by Plato as encompassing love of man for the entirety of his environment and the preservation of all that is deemed beautiful, so was libido for Freud in a more humanly circumscribed yet similarly enveloping sense. Freud's notion of libido expands beyond pure sexuality and includes a yearning for emotional gratification and a state of harmony with one's world, including one's social world. Libido is the vehicle in which one establishes and maintains contact with the good things in life. While Freud's conceptualization of libido is far more complex than mentioned here, it does have a special connection to love. Love, in my view, however, is not only an instinctual derivative as Freud presents his concept of libido to be. Love is an ego state, a condition wherein the person is in special, intimate relation to another, significant person. This relationship involves the energy of all emotions that pertain to the feeling states of loving and being loved. Libido is a mental energy that flows between two people that creates a sense of connectedness in their mutual love.

It is the libidinal relationship which will be addressed in this book. The relationship between persons within which love flows freely beckons particular attention. Psychoanalyst Michael Balint, a member of the so-called "British school" of object relations theorists who established themselves firmly in 1941, took great effort to illuminate this thing we call love , and the uniquely human relationship within which it initiates. The relationship to which Balint refers is that of the mother-infant bond. Balint believed whole heartedly that the infant is born in a state of primitive, yet potent, relationship to its environment, an experience to which he gives the aforementioned descriptive name "primary love."[1] Although Balint acknowledged that this primal relationship was not entirely inundated with blissful love, he also rightly emphasized the significance of the mother-infant bond from which emanates the infant's normative striving from birth for the love of its mother. This is a love that secures its existence through the gratification of needs and wishes, which in turn cultivates the child's developing capacity to return love and to gratify the needs and wishes of its mothering figure. From a mutuality of experience will the infant be in harmony with its environment and be capable of encountering the tenderness of love with security and serenity. Balint believed, as did his colleague Sigmund Freud and most contemporary psychoanalytic theoreticians, that it is the continued desire and yearning of persons throughout their lives to reestablish this blissful, harmonious environment as a means of securing peace, tranquility, and strength in a world beset with potential and actual threats to one's existence. The love that bonds mother and infant never ceases during the span of one's life. The foundation holds with unshakable tenacity as love's structure evolves and expands with increasing sophistication as the infant proceeds through the psychosocial developmental stages of life with the invincible memory traces of that gloriously effulgent experience of primary love.

The purpose of this book is not to recapitulate Michael Balint's psychoanalytic theoretical formulations, but to simply borrow his concept of primary love as the framework from which the courses of development of love, intimacy, and attachment will be outlined as they proceed in confluence with the overall psychosocial development of the human being. Many psychoanalytic theoreticians and clinicians have utilized Balint's concept of primary love and have expanded it to their fitting. This author will take place among them and while acknowledging indebtedness to Balint, pay homage to his hallmark contributions to the psychoanalytic movement. It shall be emphasized that this essay is not one comprised of the author's own theoretical constructs, rather it is one that acknowledges and reiterates the conceptualizations of numerous psychoanalytic theoreticians—a compilation of decades of thought that have contributed to the analytic profession's arduous, admirable, and accomplished attempt to understand the dynamics of personal and interpersonal maturation and expression in their "normality" as well as "abnormality." They have cultivated this author's thoughts incisively. Specifically, the focus of interest in this book is on love as manifested within the uniquely human sphere. This author is particularly thankful to Dr. Michael Balint's very beautifully humanistic approach to this fascinating, though elusive, subject. The author also takes stand aside all pioneering and contemporary colleagues who humbly admit the lack of definition of this thing we call love. Nonetheless, a humbly modest attempt is made herein to describe love's phenomenology and trace its development.

Indeed, love progresses and expands in experiential quality intertwined with the psychosocial development of the human person. The author has chosen to focus intently on the normative process of the development of love, with full recognition that, as the author has discovered in the clinical practice of psychotherapy, divergence from the normal process does, indeed, sadly exist. In fact, the love that is to be described may well be taken as an ideal, towards which we all benevolently strive, and of which we all to some degree fall short. This is human existence, and may it be boldly suggested that without an ideal toward which to endeavor, human experience diminishes in splendor and glory.

Chapter One

Love and the Subjective World of the Infant

To conceptualize the world of the newborn infant may well seem to be a venture in futility. Scientific investigation has not yet acquired the truth of what life is like to the newborn. The adult human mind, in all its pretentious wisdom and creativity, simply does not understand by what means the human personality develops. Psychoanalysis has to date made the most astute attempt to draw a schematic map of both the human mind and the dynamics of personal experience. But, because psychoanalysis, in theory, is not a solid investigative science, the profession can only postulate by metaphorical interpretation. The resulting allegory is, nonetheless, a tremendous and admirable stride to discover and comprehend the truth about how and why persons feel, think, and behave in the manner in which they do.

The human infant is born without a sense of time and space, and without a sense of substance and constancy. Indeed, the infant lacks a sense of *self*. The newborn is without an organized psyche or mental structure, and lives in a state of oblivion completely absorbed by its own physical state of existence. It's experiences of internal sensation and stimulation are reminiscent of its preceding intrauterine life wherein it is but a unitary, closed system enveloped by the shielding, protecting body of the mother.[1] Exposed physically to the external world upon the traumatic event of birth, the newborn struggles to sustain its internal equilibrium and maintain in this tenuous state of existence. The newborn subsists in an all encompassing, protected, self-sustaining and self-thriving system of unitary existence.

The principal force that sustains the infant's internal state of well-being is that of libido. Neonatal libido is qualitatively identical to that of libidinal life in utero, and it is precisely this biological force of energy that is the direct forerunner of what will be identified later in development as the phenomenon of love. After birth, libido flows mainly within the infant's own encapsulated body. The infant invests itself in its own bodily existence. Libido at this developmental point, due to the newborn's lack of mental, psychological structure, is strictly biological in nature. It is not yet of psychological origin and function. Libido is the physical life force that organizes and maintains the infant's sense of existence. It is noted here, and elaborated in chapter three, that the biological libido that sustains the newborn's internal sense of well-being exists only within the context of the mother-infant relationship. The facilitating role of the mother fosters the transformation of a purely biological libido to an advanced libido which includes a psychological component. It is this psychological element that soon becomes a constituent of human love.

A newborn experiences sensations that derive mainly from its internal organs and tissues and operate in interconnection with the central nervous system. Stimuli emanating from these organs and tissues provide for the infant its experiential, feeling states.[2] The infant cathects these internal states with biological libido. External stimuli that the newborn encounters are perceived as coming from within rather than from the environment. Even nourishment from mother's breast is sensed as an internal event rather than a given from the outside world. The newborn's internal stimuli consist primarily of sensations derived from the muscular movements, heartbeat, pulsation, breathing, intestinal and stomach spasms, sucking, swallowing, regurgitating, defecating, and so on. Yet, it is precisely these sensations which initiate the infant's developing awareness of time, space, continuity, and, ultimately, a sense of self. Due to cerebral immaturity and lack of experience with an objectified world, the infant's thinking is rudimentarily limited to sparsely formed islands of experience of need-tension and need-tension relief. The newborn forms vague memories of these sensations and the primitive mind registers these sensations within its developing system. Over time these experiential registrations, laid down as memory traces, sophisticate and become increasingly vivid, as well as retrievable.

The young infant's internal world may be said to consist of mainly two subject states: Tension and the associated experience of displeasure, and tension-relief and the associated experience of pleasure. Tension, as encountered by the infant, is the result of unsatisfied biological urges of which hunger is among the essential ones. Gratification and tension-relief are the result of a drive-need being reduced upon the provision of, for example, mother's nourishment. These experiential states of pleasure and displeasure are the forerunners of the development of emotions. In a short time, the infant acquires the capacity for both motility and volition, and can through various bodily and vocal movements, give cues that it is experiencing tension and seeks tension reduction. An example of this behavior is a newborn thrashing and crying out for relief of its painful experience of hunger. This state of displeasure

automatically induces the infant to retrieve memory traces of previously encountered and similar states of displeasure which serve only to intensify the
uncomfortable sensation. Upon receiving mother's nourishment and feeling
the reduction of hunger pain, the infant retrieves memory traces of this now,
pleasurable feeling. As life continues, the ongoing encounters of need-tension
followed by need-tension relief solidify the memories of displeasurable and
pleasurable experience, respectively, within the young infant's psyche. This
is how the newborn experiences life and begins to form mental structure.[3]

Humans have a relatively long weaning period before an individual is
capable of functioning fully independent of one's lifebearer and caregiver.
During this period, the infant is unquestionably dependent on its mother for
the sustenance of life biologically, psychologically, and socially. It is within
this very realm that primordial love transpires. In this scheme, the baby and
its environment, particularly with the mother, are but one entity. The child of
early infancy does not yet know the "me" from the "not me." Yet, a person,
by necessity, develops biologically, psychologically, and socially within the
context of itself and its environment. The mother, in the newborn's pliable
mind, is purely an object of its subjectivity. The infant , through the buildup
of memory traces of pleasure at the good mother's breast, develops a desire
for this object of nourishment and gratification. However, the newborn does
not yet know objectively that it is "me" who is desiring the nourishment. As
well, the infant does not yet know that it is the mother that is the source of
this nourishment.

Undifferentiated from its external world, the infant nonetheless does experience a disparate sense of separation when it feels the pangs of hunger. This
is a qualitatively new experience for the newborn having had all nourishment
supplied without summons while in utero. Hunger and its associated tension,
without immediate gratification, leaves the infant's physical and emotional
well-being out of balance, subjecting the child to pain. This sensation of
separateness is very discomforting, motivating the neonate to reach out, however nondirectionally, for its mother's ministrations. After a good feed at its
mother's breast the infant once again regains its tranquil sense of wholeness
and completeness. In time, the baby acquires the capacity to discern states of
comfort and discomfort, and learns that there are forces and functions emanating from somewhere that affect its level of comfort and thus influence its internal well-being. The young infant becomes acutely aware of its experiences
of pleasure and displeasure, and that the unpleasant experiences can indeed be
alleviated. How and why this happens the infant cannot yet conceptualize, for
its experiences remain under the rubric of its internal feelings.[4]

After repeated encounters of hunger-displeasure followed by gratification-
pleasure, the young infant continues to formulate memory traces not only of

disparate displeasurable and pleasurable feeling states, but also of sequences of, for example, the displeasure of hunger followed shortly by the pleasure of gratification. The memory traces it builds become increasingly strong and clear in the baby's mind until eventually they contribute to a newly acquired ability to perceive, however vaguely at first, and discover that external things are capable of restoring its tranquil state. This process evolves as the mother's ability and willingness to perform the necessary ministrations are carried out.

Perceptual capacity of the infant develops significantly by the age of three months. However, the image of the gratifying mother is still rather diffuse, generalized, and transient, just as is the infant's simultaneously developing sense of self. The perceptual image of the object of satisfaction is an internally derived image born from the accumulated memory traces of pleasure. These combine with the rudimentary image of the increasingly objectively perceived, external person of mother. Yet, the infant of three months still cannot objectively differentiate itself from the gratifying mother.

The perceptions of self and mother occur mainly during times of experienced need-tension, when mother's availability holds immediate meaning and value. When mother attends her baby's need, the baby highly invests its mother with libido. It is at this juncture of maturation that libido incorporates into its manifest function and service its humanistically psychological element. The infant-child has established its foundation of love. The event of libidinal investment further strengthens the image of mother and provides the baby with intense pleasure. Libido begins to turn outward from the initially physiological, internal state toward the object of the mothering person. However, upon satisfaction of need, the infant withdraws libidinal investment in the mother image and retreats into itself in a state of quiescence and contentment.

The transient perception of the mother is marked by the oscillating flow of libido to and from her in direct reflection of the child's idiosyncratic and untimely needs. To emphasize, the mother-infant relationship at this point in the child's life is primarily of a need gratifying nature, imbuing the mother and her baby's yet underdeveloped image of her with value contingent fully on her ability to meet her loved one's need for satisfaction. The mother's image is not yet fully objectified. It remains within the circumscribed subjective world of the fledgling infant-child.

From the very outset, the baby's relationship to its mother is colored significantly with pleasure. This relation, as self-gratifying to the infant as it is, sets the stage for future development of love and intimacy based on more sophisticated and intricate interactions. In essence, an unspoken dialogue, primitive yet powerful in force, is established between the infant and its mother. Because the young infant has limited control of what transpires within this dialogue, the role of the mother is vital. However, as will be elaborated in chapter three, the child does possess remarkable ability to initiate and maintain nonverbal communication and interaction with its mother.

The mother's significance in encouraging and facilitating this early dialogue is founded fundamentally on her function as need gratifyer. Her baby's physical needs are those to which the mother must be essentially attentive. By providing regular and appropriate bodily contact—holding, soothing, cleansing, and feeding—she creates a harmonious, relational matrix within which her infant internalizes the loving ministrations she offers. This process of internalization is one generated by the infant's unconscious, wishful fantasy of being pleased in emotional connection to this wonderful person not yet known. Early internalizations, under the positive valence of love, foster the development of the baby's capacity to express love and intimacy in reciprocal relationship with the mother. Mother in essence teaches her baby through her mirroring actions how to love.

The infant's internalization of the mother's love and care comes about most strongly through feeding. However, it is not merely the event of having its hunger alleviated that promotes internalization and the reciprocal flow of love and intimacy. The global, all encompassing experience of feeding includes the stimulation of all of the infant's five senses. The baby at its mother's breast feels not only relief of stomach distension, but also encounters other intensely pleasurable tactile sensations of the oral cavity—sucking with the tongue, the smacking of the lips, and the feel of the flow of warm milk through the mouth and throat. As the infant gazes into mother's eyes, she reciprocates in kind. The baby can identify the unique bodily aromas of its mother with intuitive recognition. It listens passively and gleefully to the mother's cooing, whispering, and soft singing. Above all, it is the holding pattern of the good mother that plays a facilitating role in the transfer of loving and intimating feelings to her progeny. Mother snuggles her baby and gently caresses, strokes, and rocks. What becomes internalized by the infant is not merely the sensation of satisfaction, but rather, the entirety of this event as it instills in the infant-child the sense of being loved and cherished.

The contextual gestalt of the feeding experience involving all of the infant's evolving perceptual systems formulates in the child's psyche an increasingly stable and solid sensory impression founded on earlier experienced and sparsely formed memory islands of gratification. The baby internalizes the mother's consistent ministrations and incorporates them into its evolving sense of self—a self who is loved and intimated and therefore can love and intimate in return. What is of greatest significance to the infant is that its mother is physically and emotionally available in her totality as a source of love and attachment beyond that of the mere provision of nourishment.

Because the infant's developing sense of self is a direct result of its relationship experiences, the child dimly begins to experience itself as the
recipient of mother's libidinous offerings, and therewith increases its sense
of separateness from the gratifying source. Additionally, the infant's yet diffuse sense of the self repeatedly experiences good feelings in acceptance of
the mother's loving services. These good-feeling experiences provide for
the formation of a rudimentary image or representation of the self within its
pliable mind. As a sense of a self formulates, so too, does an equally rudimentary representation of the mother. These greatly undercultivated, mental
representations of self and mother, laid down as engrams in the infant's mind,
are fused with one another. And, in the baby's mind they are identified as
the very pleasure derived from mother's gratifying offerings. Yet, because
the images of self and mother are still archaically formed, the infant is still
far from experiencing itself in full differentiation from mother, though the
process is firmly under way.[5]

Experiencing itself and maturing within the relational context of the
mother-child matrix, the infant finds itself encapsulated in a deeply emotional
relationship. Although this harmonious relationship is founded on biologically based homogeneity, the newborn also actively seeks in an equally strong
capacity the satisfaction of needs of a psychological, relational nature—specifically, love, intimacy, and attachment. The baby reaches out for more and
more experience with the mothering figure with wishful anticipation that it
will be of pleasurable quality. Parallel to its reaching out to receive love and
intimacy, the infant also extends itself to give love. The capacity to offer
intimation acquires strength and ascendency as the sense of self emerges.
Bonding between the mother and her progeny sophisticates as equally as
it maintains its tenacity and vigor. Though the quality and nature of the attachment modifies and expands in evolution, it maintains its foundation on
the primacy of love. The mother-infant bond is as emotionally intimate as a
human relationship can possibly be. Through the process of internalization
the pristine child of infancy assimilates mother in all her goodliness, and it
is mother's effective and timely caregiving that supplies the building blocks
with which her baby can construct its internal, mental world. The reward of
this developing mental domain is a mother's witness to her progeny's burgeoning sense of self.[6]

Mutual love is engendered by repeated experiences of satisfaction through
the consistent patterning of mother-child interaction. As a result, the baby
acquires an increasing sense of both trust and hope. Coming to believe in the
effectiveness and continuity of mother's loving provisions, the infant comes
to believe and have confidence in its ability to both receive and provide love.
Faith is secured in that all is well within its primal, unitary existence with the

generous mother. It is love that generates and perpetuates a mutually trusting attachment. Love's potency in this emotional experience is unquestionable and unremitting.

The faith and the hope that the infant develops within the relational matrix of itself and its mother are not simply emotional phenomena passively acquired as a given within the realm of effective mothering. Mother does in fact facilitate her baby's sense of trust and hope, however, her infant takes an active role in its procurement. As previously acknowledged, the infant is indeed completely dependent on a caretaker. Yet the infant brings with itself into extrauterine life a fundamental, yet keenly concise and efficient, repertoire of capabilities of both a physical and psychosocial nature.[7] Physically vulnerable to the onslaughts of external stimuli, the newborn is nonetheless equipped with innately endowed reflex capabilities. At birth, the primary reflex capacities are those of grasping, sucking, and looking. The newborn only hours old will, when placed at its mother's breast, automatically and intuitively turn its head, grasp hold of the breast, differentiate with its lips and tongue the nipple from its surrounding tissue, and initiate the sucking reflex. And as any mother will endearingly depose, her baby will almost invariably posit a direct gaze into her eyes. It is of interest to note that the newborn's inborn visual acuity permits it to visualize with clarity a distance of approximately eight to ten inches—precisely the typical distance between the infant's eyes and those of it's mother in the nursing position. This is nature's wondrous way at work. Eye to eye contact during the baby's earliest feedings begins the feelings of love, intimacy, and attachment more than any other event in the early psychosocial development of a human.[8]

As previously noted, the infant is acutely attuned to its five senses and utilizes them for self-preservation with remarkable precision and to engage in emotional dialogue with the mothering person for the establishment of ongoing social relations. It is necessary for the infant to take in and process external stimuli and acquire the capacity for communicative output based on internally sensed needs. This facilitates normal maturation and functioning of its neurological system. Within the accommodating matrix of mother and progeny, the infant intuitively and excitedly reaches out for external stimulation and engagement with the social being of its mother. The infant is not the passive recipient of the mother's physical and emotional supplies. Indeed, it seeks out these provisions. A baby at its mother's breast is not passively suckled, it pursues the nourishment by actively searching for and sucking at the nipple.[9]

It is this outwardly turning for vital as well as merely entertaining stimuli that constructs the foundation on which the infant itself, in the relational context of the facilitating mother, develops the capacity and propensity to love and be intimate with its mother. What starts out as an instinctual drive toward an internal state of physical equilibrium soon becomes a drive to secure and assimilate things and events from the infant's external, physical and social world. Love, intimacy, and a sense of attachment are the fuel with which the child quests.

As the infant turns increasingly outward for social interaction it develops the capacity to adapt to its expanding and highly stimulating social world. The mother filters for her baby the incoming barrage of external stimuli that would otherwise overwhelm the child and disrupt its physical and emotional well-being. However, by direct social interaction, the infant learns to assume this function for itself. It learns not only to filter overtaxing stimuli, but also to initiate increasingly complex relations, and maintain or terminate the resulting stimulation at will.[10] For example, the infant can and does initiate and terminate eye contact with its mother. While nursing, the baby will occasionally disrupt its mutual gaze with the mother and temporarily divert eye contact and attention to surrounding things and events. Conversely, the infant may temporarily cease feeding to stare inquisitively into mother's eyes and initiate the smiling reflex. The diverted interest in the entirety of mother's face, as well, unquestionably shows its love and gratitude for mother's generous provisions. The infant regulates the level of desired receptivity to being held, cuddled, and soothed by sending cues to its mother through eye contact, head turning, and vocal expression such as cooing, sighing, and crying. The child of infancy thereby actively furthers its unfolding sense of self.

It is the mother's function and task to accommodate her baby's desire and innate propensity for social interaction. She services this need with her own similarly inherent proclivity toward acknowledgment and affirmation of her beloved child. She can perceive her baby as a person in its own right and address it in this regard in all forms of interaction. The mother attunes herself to her baby's developing capacity to initiate and regulate its social activity, and adapts herself to her infant's playful and need satisfying pursuits. As the infant thrashes its body in an effort to reach out for the mother, she responds intuitively by drawing her baby's body to her own, holding and cuddling her loved one as the two reciprocate in love and intimacy. The baby will often reach for its mother's face as if to beckon her contagious smile, soothing voice, and inviting kisses. As the child embraces this precious engagement within the mother-infant matrix it learns that it has the capacity to be entertained by its mother and can, as well, entertain her.

It is indisputable that long before the human child develops the cognitive capacity to conceptualize and use language that there transpires an equally efficient communicational network mediated solely through emotional expression. The intimate, loving attachment of mother and infant is beyond reproach. To listen to the often poignant descriptions by mothers of their relationships with their babies and the latter's communicative capabilities, it is clear that an infant only weeks of age has the surprising capacity to imitate the mother's emotional expressions. The newborn possesses an amazing reflexive repertoire within the realm of its facial musculature to mimic mother's facial expressions. When mother smiles, baby smiles. When mother widens her eyes, baby reciprocates. These events are motivated by the infant's desire to interchange with the mother, and it is the same force that encourages the mother to accommodate her baby's wishes. In fact, it is impossible to determine which of the two persons initiates the pleasurably infectious imitation. Mother and infant are so enthralled by their communicative process that neither participant can resist the enticing anticipation of the other's facial response. The smile posits the most rewarding of these facial imitations, emerging around the second or third month of the infant's life. The mother's smile signifies that she is there—there within the entire realm of mothering care. The baby's smile signifies that mother's presence is acknowledged and that all is well.

This contagious form of primitive imitation is yet very rudimentarily processed within the limited intellectual sphere of the young infant because the newborn does not perceive of itself in differentiation from its mother. The young infant cannot comprehend the meaning of the mutually imitative course, yet it's potency in service to the infant in the realm of emotional experience is unquestionably profound. Love and intimacy are mediated through empathy. Empathy generates the entire spectrum of maternal support for her loved one.[11] Her maternal empathy facilitates the infant's developing love of oneself.

A sense of the self who is loving, loved, and uniquely lovable, comprises the foundation of a person who feels purpose, function, and intention. But the eventual claim of selfhood is necessarily the result of effortful and persistent socialization, a self-determined and generated engagement with the world of important, special, and facilitating persons much like whom the nascent being of the infant will in time become—a personhood to claim with individual integrity and identification. It is through this primary love and the facilitating mother that the intimate journey of livelihood proceeds.

Chapter Two

Love and Motherhood

A mother is an indispensable key to the physical and psychological well-being of her newborn infant. Acknowledging her baby as a burgeoning being, the mother may realize her roles as both mediator and buffer between her newborn and the complex, overwhelming world. It is the mother who eventually introduces this world to her infant as well as nurtures the infant to become itself. This gradual process imbues the mother with a profound influence and responsibility. Caring for a fully dependent newborn, to which any parent will attest, is no simple matter. Motherhood can create great emotional, mental, and physical vulnerability for a woman. It is a very taxing job with far reaching ramifications for both the child and parent. Yet most mothers assume this role with goodwill and seemingly instinctual certainty. While a mother's benevolence is typically unwavering, the ease with which she consciously chooses motherhood varies.

Love, ideally, plays an integral role in procreation and the crucial experiences of mothering. Her pregnancy is fraught with ambivalence and high hopes in procreation, of presenting to the world a person of her own flesh and blood. On the other side of the coin lurks fear. A prospective mother may not help but fear in some vague but real sense the birth of her child. There is potential for danger to herself, her baby, and perhaps to the personalized, social world which she has developed with great care.

Mature adults accept one another in matrimony with the hopes of growing emotionally and spiritually, individually and as a couple. Most couples choose to express themselves in this growth through the creation of a human being who will represent and symbolize the mutual love of their union. It is with this binding love and intimacy that the woman may fantasize about the creation and life of their child. In pronouncement of the love which transpires within, and is contained by, the union of their marriage, the woman wishes not just for a child, but for a child with and through her husband. This child shall be conceived in love. By means of this fantasy the woman can consciously wish for the reproduction of herself as well as of her cherished partner. She desires to declare herself, her husband, and their relational bond.

The woman's inherent need to reproduce is multifaceted. Many women wish to reproduce both as an expression of love in marriage and as a desire to regenerate herself and the man she loves. This desire and expression is unquestionably the result of a combination of psychological, social, and cultural determinants. Question arises as to how much of this maternal urge is instinctually and biologically driven. Maternal instinct cannot be denied. A person need only to observe the tie between a mother and her child, especially during its infancy.[1] The synchronicity with which mother and baby interact leaves no doubt that both the mother and child are biologically driven to generate transaction. An early expression of the maternal instinct occurs at puberty. Female adolescents often experience a variety of feelings associated with both conscious and unconscious fantasies of mothering. These feelings are heightened with the beginning of menstruation and the feelings are typically experienced with anxiety. Anxiety is the foundation of the ensuing ambivalence with which most women view both menstruation and reproduction. It can be argued that biological, hormonal factors meet with psychological and sociocultural influences in a woman's desire to procreate.

Traditional psychoanalytic thought states that the instinct that drives women to reproduction is "masochistic" and is found in both the biological and psychological makeup of the entire gender. It is theorized that "feminine masochism" is defined by the psychological upheaval during pregnancy and the pain of birthing.[2] Additionally, mother bears the emotional pain of the series of losses resulting from the psychological and social maturation of her offspring. Beginning with the separation from mother's womb at birth, children progressively detach from their mothers. The closeness of prenatal and immediate postnatal attachment between a mother and her child is relatively short-lived. Mothers bear the brunt of separation as the child grows.

Is this passivity a natural course of wifehood and motherhood? Historically, maybe. However, contemporary women have assumed a more active role in their sexuality, marriage, and mothering. Reproduction is no longer a natural consequence of sexual intercourse, but a conscious choice. The modern, ideal marriage is based on a functional interdependence between the two partners and less on traditionally dominant and submissive roles. Mothers are freer to delegate some of the parental responsibilities to husbands and caretaking professionals. In conversation with pregnant women and mothers of newborns, it is obvious that motherhood and mothering are not purely passive and masochistic in nature. Women speak freely of the joy and exhilaration they feel upon learning of their impregnation and the anticipation of creating one with oneself. Sexuality during the family planning stage is frequently more intense for women hoping for conception. A woman may be absorbed by her emotions, awaiting the fruit of the intimacy between her and her lover and the intimacy she may experience with a baby. Women can be more free for expression of love, as well as more free from anxiety, during the family planning stage of sexuality with their husbands. Women speak of the solidification of the attachment between them and their husbands even though they are free to devote much of their love to their child.

Motherhood does entail a physical and emotional pain that has an unavoidable masochistic quality. The pain is nonetheless an anticipation of suffering, the deprivation of a mother's comfort in the service of her motherly aspiration. The results of which are the joys that can only be described and understood by other mothers. This joy is unique to her fellow woman, as well as unique to her own individuality.

For many, motherhood is the most intense and enriching experience of life. Founded on their own loving infantile experiences, the earliest wishes for love and intimacy remain with women through their entire lives. These wishes form ideals for a mutuality—the notion of loving and being loved and of nurturing and being nurtured. Wishing to recreate her own intimacy, it can be ultimately achieved by bearing and mothering an infant of her own. Both the nature and quality of a mother's relationship with her newborn are profoundly influenced by her own earliest experiences. The mother relives the harmonious union of infancy with the roles this time reversed. The intimacy is recaptured and she can seize the opportunity to become the "good" mother that her mother was to her. It is an identification with her own mother that offers her a foundation from which she learns what a good mother should be.

A maternal identity is something a woman acquires in the process of being mothered herself. A woman learns to mother by being mothered.[3] She establishes an ideal for herself in early childhood which takes the form of a value system. A young woman invests considerable energy in striving to reach this ideal, to be like her mother in goodliness as a mother, as well as in her identification with her mother's femininity. A mother's femininity is one that attracts the good man like the girl's father. A maturing child will accept her femininity and upon reaching adulthood, desire to experience it in many ways, including that of motherhood.

By bearing a child, a woman can experience and strengthen her sense of femininity. However, femininity crystalizes only as a woman simultaneously relinquishes her infantile dependency and solidifies her identification with her own mother as her own autonomously functioning woman who can love and be loved by a man, as well as bear a child with him. It is the totality of a woman not only as an adequate, mature lover and effective mother, but also as a person who aspires for good things, that can make a woman feel complete, valued, and well adapted to reality. Motherhood is only one position on a spectrum of life, but one that holds great potential for helping a woman link her past and her present in preparation for the future, as well as ease through unresolved conflicts in interpersonal relationships and self-esteem. Any woman who can bear the emotional and physiological changes in the entirety of the reproductive process has prevailed over perhaps the most challenging of all human tasks.

An emotionally intense attachment between spouses crystalizes with sexual intercourse as the person of each lover is internalized and becomes integrated into the self of the other. Impregnation ensues and actualizes the wondrous event of conception. This achievement fulfills the ultimate aim of coitus during the family planning stage for both partners — to reproduce the selves of both, as well as to pronounce in representational form the matrimonial union at perhaps its peak of intimacy. The woman achieves the original and eternal wish to reestablish in her own womb the mystical union that was experienced in her mother's womb. The embryo is, from the mother's perspective, at one not only with herself but the bond of wife and husband. Upon learning of conception, a woman often feels a sense of estrangement not yet firmly colored with either a positive or negative impression. She may find it difficult to envision herself instilled with the power of motherhood. The experience of estrangement is not only from the world of which she is a part, but also from her own sense of self. A woman can expect to experience feelings of depersonalization, of no longer being the person of whom she has thought and experienced herself to be.[4] Understandably, the person of the pregnant woman is no longer the person she once was. She undergoes an immediate personal change, an experience which only another mother can explain.

Estranged from her usual self and surrounding world, the future mother may yet feel at one with the universe. She becomes the connection of past to future. In a more immediate sense she extends the generational bond between her mother and herself to the next generation in the motherhood cycle. A generational link is reestablished as a transcendence from womb to womb. The picture is no longer of "mother and myself," but becomes "mother and myself, the mother." This sudden cognizance is a profoundly significant epiphany for a woman.

Both physically and psychologically, a woman must integrate the life of her unborn child into her own sense of the self. She finds herself in the midst of physiological transformation of the endocrinological system as well as one of the body as a whole. Her biggest challenge is that of redistributing her physical, mental, and emotional energy into essentially three arenas. As a wife, she continues to invest herself in both her husband and their relationship. The relationship itself undergoes a qualitative change upon learning of her pregnancy to which both partners must adjust. With the support of her husband, the future mother may not only adapt to but initiate a redistribution of libidinal investment.

This is the second arena of energy redistribution. A mother-to-be is no longer responsible only to herself, but to another whose needs to some degree are different from her own. Her embryo is more fragile than is she. The woman's sense of autonomy must strengthen to support not only herself, but her embryo. Initially, this may be a difficult task for the woman who may not have yet fully grasped the presence of another being within herself. This leads to the third arena in which the woman must invest herself. She relates to her unborn child with loving energy, learning how to love in a qualitatively different way than ever before. This task she must accomplish on her own terms. It is the future mother's very sense of personhood that, in its ultimately unique form, must create its similarly unique loving attachment to her progeny. Beyond the three arenas, a woman ideally maintains interest and energy in all other realms of her life that also provide the additional affirmation needed in her pursuit of motherhood.

In fantasy, the triadic family unit is established — mother, father, and child. It is the fulfillment of this wishful fantasy for which the mother-to-be longs with the promise of its realization in the foreseeable future. This fantasy is one that will indeed materialize, the quality of which she does not yet know, but the hopes for which she crystallizes with endearment.

Upon giving birth, the newborn is greeted with mother's ecstasy and hope that has generated inside her for nine months. The mother's highly circumscribed world is vested with a love and intimation engendered deeply within her person. In her mind, she may be at one with the world, a world that exists at that point exclusively for her child.[5] A mother is not only the carrier, but an all encompassing reservoir of love. The love already invested in the marriage is temporarily diverted to the mother's newborn child. This child is her wondrous product, a derivative of her own flesh and blood, and one that pronounces with resonance her achievement. The sheer power of the birthing experience permeates the mother's soul, renewing her own sense of being born. She is a new and different person living in a world equally new and different. The new mother tends to her creative planning for the future and what it may hold for her expanded family circle. Her life is in complete reorganization as she orients herself to a fresh view of personal and social being.

The mother, as the primary representation of the external world, wishes to promote an environment as close in nature as possible to that of the infant's intrauterine life. She does this not only to protect her child, but to give her value as a protecting mother and to maintain her personal integrity. Captivated and charmed by her infant, the mother continues to emotionally invest her child as a part of herself, just as the child was in utero.[6] What was mystically created by nature for her, and embodied within during gestation, the mother wishes to reestablish in close proximity postpartum. She desires to maintain the blissful union that is yet in the prime of its existence. This serves not only to protect her newborn, but also the psychological investment the mother has in her child. The physical separation at birth can be just as traumatic for the mother as it is for the newborn. However differently this event of separation is experienced, many new mothers cannot help but to suffer emotional losses from the birth of the child once a part of herself. Fortunately, this separation is expected. Ideally, a mother-to-be prepares herself for this loss. Preparing for the establishment of a new relationship with her baby, a mother facilitates for herself, psychologically, as smooth a transitional process as possible for childbirth. The emotional loss incurred with parturition is ameliorated to a significant extent, and compensated for, by the gift of the observable person now divested of its mystery. Giving birth, for many women, begins actualization — seeing, hearing, and touching her progeny. In effect, a mother discovers her child to no longer be a fantasy, but a reality.[7]

The reality of her creation is crystalized when the newborn is placed into her inviting arms. A mother will visually scan her baby until finally fixating her gaze on the infant's face. She so very gently caresses her progeny while softly touching and stroking its face and head with her fingertips. Vital bodily contact is established and therewith the infant begins the long, tenuous journey into personhood. The mother is there to facilitate this process. The infant's instinctual aim is for nourishment, nourishment within the providing context of love, intimacy and attachment. A blissful, ecstatic relationship is underway based on mutual satisfaction formulating a uniquely precisional fit between mother and newborn. Every aspect of this extremely emotional relationship, as well as of all other interactions, captures the mother's attention and occupation. The mother-infant relationship is the center of the mother's interest and devotion. The father is joyfully and curiously, yet often apprehensively, drawn to this relational bond, and it becomes his task to support and confirm the mother in her critical role. A mother may summon the support of her husband in the care of both herself and their child, and receive him in confirmation of the love and intimacy that has culminated in the very creation of a child.

Upon close observation of the primal relationship of mother and infant it is clear the mother grasps even more fully the reality of her child. The baby, no longer an imaginary being, commands recognition of its pronounced presence in all realms of its needs and wishes. The mother devotes herself unselfishly to her infant's yearnings. The recognition of her baby's needs is mediated by the process of identification. A motherly woman immediately identifies with herself as a person who desires love and affection. She receives this from her baby and her husband, and is thereby deemed a lovable person. Also, at a very conscious level, a mother may identify herself with the universality of all mothers. However, much more potently, a mother may identify with her new-born in three ways: She identifies with her infant itself; she identifies with her own mother and the way the latter had mothered her; and she identifies with an ideal notion of motherhood of which her own mother was deemed to have fallen short. This latter identification is rooted in early infancy, ingrained into the psyche of the infant and sustained in the unconscious mind as the child matures to adulthood and her own motherhood. It is this maternal ideal that, in intricate connection with her actual infantile experiences and the way the woman, now matured, views her own mother, provides the driving force with which she pursues her motherly functions in service of her infant's needs and wishes. The three dimensions of identification will now be elaborated.

A mother intuitively identifies with her baby and how it experiences itself in its early-life state. She accomplishes this by retrieving vague, yet stable, memory traces of her own experiences in the infantile position a generation ago. If in the mother's infantile experiences she was provided effective, loving care within the realm of genuine empathy by her own mother, these experiences formulate as an integral component of the maturing woman's evolving personality, to be freely expressed in like fashion in interaction with her baby. The mother freely provides loving service because she freely received it in her own infancy and childhood. The effective mother nurses and holds her baby as she was nursed and held in her early life. She recaptures the experience of being an infant well taken care of and now shares with her progeny the experience of having a loving mother. The mother sees herself as a good mother and acquires confidence in her motherliness.

The second dimension of identification by which a mother displays genuine empathy and concern for her infant is by consciously perceiving the motherly nature of her own mother. Experiences of being mothered are internalized by the child and become an integral part of her personality. As the child matures, she recalls actual interactions and situations in her life in relationship with her mother and forms identifications with these internalized experiences. These identifications serve as the prototype for all future relations with her mother as well as with significant others, including her own child.

A young daughter learns from her mother's characteristics the quality of interpersonal relations. She plays "house" with her dolls, and plays out her fantasies of being a loving mother to her own baby. A mother is conditioned to effectively care for her infant under the positive valence of love through the identification process. A mother is capable of and oriented to mothering her child with an unqualified sense of intimation and attachment. This is facilitated by the polarized identification with both her infant and her mother. There remains, however, an integrating phenomenon which comprises the third dimension of identification. This phenomenon is the ultimate expression of the mother's unique personality and connects the two aforementioned poles of identification. The maternal ideal, as earlier mentioned, is the integrating component of the identification process inherent in all mothering occasions. A partly conscious and partly unconscious phenomenon, the maternal ideal is that which the mother has fantasized since early childhood regarding how she would have ideally wished her mother to have been, and how she would have ideally wished to have been mothered. At a purely conscious level every woman (and man) has, in actual interaction with her mother, a fantasied version of what would have ideally transpired in the mother-child relation, and that would have provided the ultimate experience of love. As conscious as these fantasies are, they have their origin, however, in infancy and are therefore grounded, in part, in the unconscious realm of experience.

The infant, in encounter with the internal, subjective states of displeasure, wishfully fantasizes about receiving its mother's loving offerings. These wishful fantasies remain within the unconscious of the infant and through childhood and adolescence. These unconscious, infantile fantasies of undisrupted pleasure intertwine with the qualitatively same fantasies that formulate later in the realm of consciousness. Only when the child has maturationally acquired the cognitive capacity to conceptualize his or her needs and wishes, and can acknowledge their presence, do the fantasies become progressively conscious. The child then becomes aware, with increasing precision, of what is deemed missing in his or her loving relation to the mother that would otherwise create an ideal situation. The unconscious wishful fantasies integrate with the later, conscious wishful fantasies to constitute for the child, the maternal ideal.

All females who elect motherhood strive for achieving the maternal ideal. No mother can accommodate her child's every wish and demand, as much as she would like to. No mother is perfect because no person is perfect, nor is any relationship perfect. Therefore, an ideal is erected between a mother and her child in their loving relation toward which all mothers strive to provide for their infant in an uncompromising experience of pleasure. She will, as did her own mother, fall short of this ideal.

Chapter Three

Love and the Mutuality of Mother-Infant Experience

Enraptured by the very essences of her own flesh, heart, and soul, a new mother embraces her progeny with an enveloping love that is as powerful as any force that prevails on this earth. The nature of this love is profoundly new and different to the mother. Blessed with the birth of her child, a mother's experience of love peaks. This is a love she shares with her husband. The arrival of their cherished baby substantiates and consolidates the marital bond. Hence is established the triadic family unit.

Yet, mother and infant begin as one, and through the mutuality of their experience shall come forth the budding person of the child who, under the auspices of love, announces and pronounces a self directly reflective of the loving mother and the environment she has created. The emergence of the infant's sense of self is mirrored by the mother whose loving qualities become an integral part of the child's personality. The infant takes an active role in helping the mother establish herself as a mirroring agent. An infant's developing perception of itself as a loving and lovable being is exacted by the intricate mutuality of the mother-infant experience.

A new mother may digress from the reality of her previously established world in service to her newborn. She constructs a circumscribed world wherein she and her baby nestle to form their unique fit, and from which they can proceed in their relationship relatively uninterrupted. Mother and infant compliment one another rather skillfully as they meld into a pleasurable state of oneness. Mutual pleasure is observable to the outside investigator, however its potency is manifested deeply within the mother and her progeny.

A mother's consistency and dependability in caring for her child is experienced by the infant as being an actual part of itself. This self will develop the capacity to relate lovingly to its mother. Primary love is founded on the availability of a mother who is taken for granted because, in the infant's view, her provisions function as a part of its developing sense of self.[1] In essence, an infant's love for its mother is based on the acquisition and maintenance of its internal sense of well-being. The infant's motive is by nature's way self-gratifying. Yet, the mother's motive, too, is self-serving, but in an equally normal and healthy manner. She seeks gratification as well and it can be found in the love she experiences with her baby. The infant, as noted, views its mother as a subjective object of pleasure. The mother views her young child as an extension of herself—a personalized being there to fulfill her biological tendencies and psychological wishes to love and be loved in vicarious recapitulation of the primacy of her own life.[2]

In the mutuality of mother-infant experience, each partner invests in the other a love that returns to and replenishes the self. Self-love and self-gratification transpire simultaneous to love for, and the wish to gratify, the other. Giving and receiving are synonymous in experience. The infant who reaches out to engage its mother in solicitation of libidinous offerings simultaneously libidinizes itself. The baby becomes a loving being and in turn feels loved, lovable, and ultimately gratified. The mother has heightened feelings of motherliness and self-esteem. She, too, feels loved, lovable, and therewith gratified in her desires for attachment, warmth, and a sense of oneness with her baby. Both mother and child feel an assurance of security and well-being as the loving relation maintains its potency.

Both mother and infant elicit from each other pleasurable feelings of satisfaction. Distinct as these two persons are, they simultaneously serve as extensions of one another.[3] Each employs the other as a facilitating tool with which to enrich and expand his or her own subjective, internal states, enhancing their ability to love and intimate in their shared experience. It is precisely this state of oneness that paradoxically accentuates the mother's perception of herself as a meritous individual in differentiation from, yet in supplementation to, the infant of her own creation. The mother who provides a holding environment for her baby, facilitates the child's increasing perception of its burgeoning self as distinct from, yet dependent on, its mother.

Maintaining the equilibrium of the mother-infant mutuality requires the accommodating roles of both parties. Both wish to preserve the well-being and cohesion that promote their active involvement, each serving the nutriment that affirms the existence of the other. They sustain their relationship through mutual cueing and response, and mold and shape one another for their individual needs and wishes.[4]

Affective dialogue is established between the mother and her beloved baby. With exquisite sensitivity, mother reads discriminatingly and accurately the readiness of her child to enlist her in emotional and social interplay. The infant sets the pace for emotional communication with its mother and her ministrations. As a mother cares for her child she adapts to its rhythmic pace, and the infant, in turn, adjusts its measure to accommodate the mother's adaptive efforts. Each partner in essence prepares for the preparedness of the other. This intricate sense of mutuality is accomplished under the aegis of mother's empathy for her baby, promoting the infant's capacity to draw from her what it currently needs and desires. The infant's ability to invite interventions from its mother by means of emotional expression further draws the mother into empathic engagement. The mother's excitement in turn entices her baby to further the emotional dialogue. Affective contagion spreads as mother and infant bask in mutual love and intimacy.

As noted earlier, the newborn's ability to think and conceptualize is extremely rudimentary, limited to the experience of unconscious, wishful fantasies. These fantasies are of gratification by means of being fed, held, and soothed by the unconditionally loving mother. Therefore, empathy manifested by the infant is based essentially on the experience of emotional attachment. Yet, as primitive as the infant's cognitive capacity is, it nonetheless learns that it has the ability to send cues to mother that will effectively elicit specifically desired responses. An infant selectively signals to its mother what it desires, and that which it vaguely yet efficiently remembers having received from her in repeated past experiences. Retrieval from memory advances the infant's capacity to determine preferentially, what provisions it seeks. A state of anticipation ensues for the baby awaiting the mother's response. This anticipatory state furthers the infant's gradually developing cognitive ability to differentiate itself from its mother and establish boundaries between the notions of me and not me.

The interchange evolves and the infant learns not only that mother can accommodate its needs and wishes, but also that it can accommodate itself to the needs and desires of mother. The infant tunes in to its mother's signals that indicate her availability and willingness to engage in interaction and emotional communication. Adapting readily to mother's cues, baby learns when the time is appropriate to request mother's attention, and conversely, when to delay its bid for attention until its mother's receptivity is primed. The mother learns in like fashion when to solicit her baby's attention. What ensues is a timely, rhythmic oscillation between attention and non-attention between the two persons necessary for the physical and psychological well-being of both. Continuity and consistency are important in the mutual adaptation in order for the infant to increase and sharpen its sensitivity to its mother as the empathic, gratifying person she is, and to conduct the mode of relationship that provides for the continuous flow of love and intimacy. The infant becomes aware of its own ever widening emotional experience.

The reciprocal flow of love and intimacy provides the infant a sense of trust in its mother's availability. Mother welcomes her baby's contagious smile and babbling vocalizations as it attempts to talk to her. This beckons her to smile responsively and, in mimicking fashion, converse with her infant. In doing so, the mother conforms to her baby's ability to effect communication. She meshes her needs and desires with those of her child as she softens the tone of her voice and slightly raises her vocal pitch to capture her baby's attention. This ongoing process facilitates her infant's developing sense of potential influence on its social world. It comes to recognize that it has the power to extract from its mother that which it deems necessary to sustain its overall well-being. Moreover, the infant acquires a vitally new function and purpose—to elicit from its mother that which will ensure its value as a lovable being. In the infant's mind it actually creates, by its own strivings for love and intimacy, the social world of its mother and the articulately woven mutuality of the mother-infant responsiveness in a loving, affective dialogue.

With the unfolding of reciprocating relations with its mother, the infant furthers its awareness of what it needs and longs for, and which responses from its mother will meet these needs and wishes. It takes form through a series of primitive yet effective thought processes with the facilitating assistance of its mother. Using the example of the infant's need for warmth and bodily contact, the course is as follows: A) The infant becomes aware of its internally experienced need-tension based on a vague sense of separateness and detachment from the mother. Separation anxiety is heightened. B) The infant determines whether the time is right to seek its mother's bodily contact. It accomplishes this by intuitively tuning in to mother's own particular needs and attention at the moment. C) Determining that its timing is right, the infant sends cues and signals to mother informing her of its needs and wish for contact. The baby learns from experience which cues and signals to deliver, for example, crying and reaching out with its arms and legs in attempt to grasp and embrace its mother. D) The infant waits with anticipation and predictability mother's forthcoming response. E) The mother, reciprocally in tune to her loved one's needs, recognizes her infant's particular call of distress and makes herself available to respond. F) She picks up her discomforted child and holds her loved one, alleviating the tension and separation anxiety. The mother secures for herself a sense of confidence in having the ability to respond empathically and effectively to her child.

It may well be noted, however, to which any mother can attest, that her baby's needs and wishes do not always take the form of an anticipatory request. Rather, infants by their dependent nature often express their needs with expectation and demand, regardless of the mother's availability and preparedness. An infant's demand is an extremely trying event for the mother. Not all of her baby's distresses can be alleviated. Colic, teething pain, discomfort from viruses and infections, and so on, are matters that a mother cannot immediately resolve. Yet, the infant will maintain complete trust in its mother if she is capable of bearing with and containing her infant's distress without losing her own confidence in her ability to provide a holding environment for her defenseless one. If mother succeeds, her baby is much more capable of enduring its discomfort. In fact, the inevitable distress actually strengthens the trust and assurance the infant has in its mother as a person who is at least there in the infant's time of adversity.[5]

Fortunately, most mothers are available and proficient in attending their loved one's distress most of the time. A mother is aware of her necessary role in providing physical and psychological care. Equally, the empathic mother is aware of her infant's need and right to experience periods of solitude. Periodically, the infant needs to disengage its mother and others, tuning in to its internal sensations as they exist independent of mother's presence. The infant can, then, further develop its sense of self and experience its unique livelihood as a person. In a state of quiescence, a baby is free to experience the very genuine sensations, impulses, and urges that establish the foundation for its emerging sense of personhood.[6] The infant does indeed require and desire the attendance of its mother to share in these experiences. However, she must allow her infant to set the timing for engagement and disengagement. The intuitive mother enlists the assistance of her infant's signaling. A baby will let its mother know when it needs undisturbed solitude. When being alone reaches the point of inducing separation anxiety and threatens its sense of attachment, the infant signals its distress to summon the mother.

In addition to its privacy in times of solitude, the infant uses times of quiet, alert inactivity to explore the surrounding inanimate world, as well as its own body parts. Alone, the infant has no difficulty in engaging itself in play.[7] Baby sucks its thumb, shifts its body, watches its hands and feet as they move about, gazes at surrounding objects, listens to external sounds as well as those emanating from within its own body. During states of solitude an infant will fantasize, however primitively, about pleasurable experiences of the past with mother. In time, the baby learns to entertain and gratify itself through self-play and exploration. However, it is the mother's acknowledged nearness, even when the infant is alone, that facilitates its expanding ability to regulate an internal sense of well-being. Indeed, it is the infant who experiences itself. Any activity the baby initiates and enjoys on its own accord is appreciated and acknowledged by the observant mother. Her response to her baby's newly acquired repertoire of behaviors serves as a mirror to the infant focusing, synthesizing, integrating, and defining its experiences and giving them personal and social meaning.[8] This, in turn, imbues her infant with a sense of value, intention, and purpose for its own existence, along with a new awareness that it has an impact on its social world.

A mother's mirroring activity is one of intuition and natural desire for intimate, loving contact with her progeny. Universally, mothers tend to imitate their babies' facial and vocal expressions, promoted by their inherent motherliness, natural inquisitiveness, identification with the child, and above all, the love for the primal beings of their own flesh and soul.

A mother's role as a mirror, reflecting the expanding experiences of her baby, is critical to the infant's increasing repertoire of feelings, thoughts, and behaviors. The infant's evolving conceptualization of a self is based firmly on its experiences as a self-initiator of these personal experiences. Responses that the infant actively elicits from its mother, particularly in the realm of emotional expression and the attitudes they imply—such as smiling as an indication of love and gratitude—are of particular significance to the infant's developing self. Emotional interaction reveals to the baby that it is both a loved and loving being. For example, when a mother holds and cuddles her infant, its emerging self is experienced with a sense of warmth, tenderness, security, and love. In time, the infant learns that it has the capacity to produce these pleasant sensations. Additionally, the infant internalizes a part of its mother's self that she wishes to share with her beloved child as a loving and lovable mother.

In order for her baby to integrate its mother's attributes, she must feel good about herself as a person and as an effective mother. The mother who witnesses her infant maturing in health and happiness with a sense of personal good feeling, will take pride in knowing that she has facilitated this growth. And the fledgling child will integrate feeling good about itself with feeling good about its mother.

Mother and infant mesh a special relationship which both cherish and neither wish to relinquish. However, nature takes its course and in the inevitable event of repeated, minor disruptions in the otherwise harmonious experience, the infant gradually disengages from union with the mother in favor of forming an identification with her. The infant wishes to become like its mother in all her goodliness. The pleasing aspects of the mother's loving care are internalized by the child and formulate part of its personality. The developing internal structure is increasingly capable of independently providing the services that mother has granted as an auxiliary self to her baby. An infant's self readily expands and sophisticates, and the mother who is initially valued by her infant for her mere service as a need gratifyer becomes a personified object with which to imitate and identify.

It is the imperative task of a mother to facilitate her child's evolution towards independence. Paradoxically, autonomy is both a sad and joyous experience for her. She transfers her caretaking functions to her child, encouraging her loved one to exercise such functions for itself. This is a process that unfolds through the developmental course of early motherhood. For example, early in infancy when a mother holds, cuddles, and rocks her newborn, soothingly talks and sings to her child, and gratifies her progeny with nourishment, she is not merely providing these loving services because of her infant's inherent dependence on her, but is in fact simultaneously preparing herself and her infant for further maturation. The mother who feels comfortable and free from conflict in facilitating her child's normative growth and maturation appreciates her infant's achievements and libidinizes these successes. Her infant enjoys and values its new adaptive capabilities.

Internalizing the mother's services and being able to sooth and contain oneself when in distress is a natural yet difficult process for the infant. To assist in effecting this process, the infant through very early childhood makes use of inanimate objects such as a soft blanket or stuffed animal to create a psychological bridge between itself and its mother. These are known as "transitional objects."[9] The child cuddles, rocks, and coos the transitional object, comforting the object as its mother would comfort her child. Thus, in mother's absence, the child learns to mother itself. Parallel to this experience, the infant itself feels comforted by the soft object as if it were, and in wishful fantasy is, the mother's own warm body. From the infant's perspective, the mother is never fully absent. The transitional effect of the so called "security blanket" or stuffed animal serves to sooth the child in its growing awareness that its mother and itself are two distinct beings. The infant's fanciful yet effective relationship with the transitional object serves to alleviate the child's separation anxiety, thereby sustaining the infant's internal well-being in its mother's absence. Thus, the infant maintains a sense of control over itself and its feelings, as well as the mother whose presence is needed in either reality or temporary illusion.

By the age of eight months the infant has developed a fundamental capacity to perform for itself much of the psychological functioning mother has provided. An eight month-old baby can, to varying degrees of success, temporarily replace maternal soothing with its own rudimentary mental activity. An essential developmental achievement is accomplished by acquiring the mental capacity to register, retrieve, and integrate memories of past gratifying encounters with its loving mother. At this maturational stage, the infant is capable of more objectively perceiving the object of its mothering figure and recognizing the specific functions she serves.[10] The mother's inevitable absences from her baby will ideally occur in optimal doses and promote her loved one's capacity to sooth itself in the midst of separation anxiety. The natural course of development for the infant effects the maturational

formation of an internal, mental image of the mother.[11] The mental image
or representation is based in formulation on early, increasingly strengthened
and sophisticated memory registers of the loving mother and her soothing
functions, and assists the infant in sustaining its sense of security and personal viability with increasing acknowledgment that itself is a being separate
from the being of its mother. The mental world of the infant expands to include something beyond a simple relation to a gratifying source, to include
a relation to an internalized mothering agency more articulate, defined, and
functional in its service. This is an internal agency that manifests itself in the
infant's burgeoning sense of self.

It is a maturational achievement for the infant to perceptually distinguish
itself from its mother and form a distinct, though not yet fully sustaining ,
internal representation of her. The infant in the second half of its first year no
longer views itself in complete merger with its mother, but as a being living in
accompaniment with her. The mother accepts this new, advanced relationship
even though it entails an inherent loss for her—the loss of the harmonious
feeling of oneness with her beloved progeny. She allows her infant to perform
the self-regulating tasks for which the child acquires increasing capacity.
However, this loss simultaneously heralds a qualitatively new sense of joy
and pride for the mother as she witnesses her baby's triumphs and mastery.
The infant's personal ascendency at this developmental juncture manifests
itself primarily in the realm of self-initiating behavior, self-soothing and
regulating service, and the containment of its separation anxiety. These acquisitions are precariously established during late infancy, yet potent in their
promise for an individuated future. The mother acquires an assurance of her
effectiveness as a loving and providing maternal figure.

As the infant's internal representation of its mother strengthens, the loving
attachment to her energizes and vitalizes. The attachment not only sustains,
but enriches, even in mother's absences, during which the infant's internal representation of the mother is cathected libidinally. It is true, as the adage suggests, that, "absence makes the heart grow fonder." Indeed, the maternal representation marks a yet primitive conceptualization for the infant; however, its
efficacy in emotional experience is undeniable. In fact, as the infant becomes
increasingly aware of its separation from the loving and beloved mother, it
acknowledges its concomitant dependence on her as an outside force that provides what the child so very much needs and desires. The infant forever longs
for its mother and her generous love because it is realized that mother, even at
a distance, nurtures its sustaining sense of security and wellness.

Chapter Four

Love and Fatherhood

Most women who choose the experience of motherhood hope to conceive their child in love. A woman's desire for a child is a manifestation of not only her hopes and dreams, but an expression of the love that she holds for her mate. Although the mothering experience is one of profound meaning and expression for a woman, she alone cannot replace or separate herself from the importance of father. The world of the mother is to great extent a derivative and reflection of the world of the father, and vice versa. Both conscious and unconscious desires of the woman and man in love mesh to create a mutual declaration of their love through the production of a child. From this perspective, the father's position—his role in this prodigious marvel—cannot be renounced.

Through the entire course of parenthood, especially in the early stage, the wife and husband serve as mirrors to one another. The mirrored image of each reflects and provides the parental pair the mutual support and affirmation that they need. From the beginning the partners enter a critical phase of personality development, both individually and as marital partners.[1] Effective parenting, as commonly understood, is a combined effort of both the mother and father in united responsibility. The partnership evolves harmoniously in the mutual gesture and response, the give and take of a relationship in which both partners are free to express their most intimate desires, fantasies, and fears concerning their impending parenthood. The emotional experiences are highly charged for both the woman and man as they engage their mothering and fathering pursuits. The intensity of the emotions experienced is compounded by the newness of the event—an awareness of their own biological and psychological thrust toward perhaps the most creative and personally intrinsic task they may face during the entire course of their lives.

The personalities of both mother and father expand maturationally as they advance to a higher level of organization. Their personalities definitively, structurally, and experientially differ from the personalities of their earlier preparenthood lives, and they must be prepared for the impending changes.[2] They must also be prepared to assimilate the advancement of their personalities, as anxiety producing as it may be, to reap the rewards of personal expansion and enrichment as well as of interpersonal involvement that is much more intimate in experience. The new mother may experience a wealth of emotions, some welcomed and some very disquieting. The multitude of feelings can amalgamate into a morass of bewilderment, leaving the woman by nature's way exalted and joyous, yet frightened and anxious. Nonetheless, she adapts to the perplexing experience, and it is the indispensable father who supports her struggle to effectively accommodate her internal changes. The father's experience compliments that of his wife's, although he obviously does not undergo the physiological changes induced by the growing fetus that the mother does. The emotional experience of the man in the pre-stages of fatherhood is of a qualitatively different nature. Nonetheless, it is uncanny yet fascinating to witness the distinct events that coincide between the soon-to-be parents.

The father is subjected to a myriad of emotions during the planning, pregnancy, birthing, and postpartum periods of his wife's motherhood. These feelings are perplexing and seemingly contradictory. Inspired by both fear and hope, the prospective father experiences a variety of fantasies about his unborn child. His fantasies and emotions manifest themselves in a variety of bodily experiences. These experiences are unexpectedly similar to the physiological changes of the gestating woman. A husband may encounter sensations such as stomach upsets, headaches, unusual eating habits, and physical and emotional fatigue. It is beyond doubt that these symptoms are an expression of the husband's identification with and concern for his wife's changes and well-being. Born out of unquestionable love for his wife, the symptoms also represent the man's both conscious and unconscious desire to be at one with her. To actualize for himself that which his wife is going through in as close a capacity as biologically possible, the husband provides for himself a sense of personal security and value in his effort to preserve himself, his wife, and the developing dyad of mother and fetus. Additionally, the husband's symptoms vicariously establish and represent his desired position in the new family unit that will soon become a reality.

The adult man also has prenatal and postnatal origins in his own early, intimate biological dependency on his mother. As discussed earlier in chapter three the relationship between mother and infant fosters the formation within the developing mind of the infant of memory traces that evolve into increasingly articulate representations of experiences of love and intimacy while being at one with the mother. These representations of biological disposition expand and manifest themselves leading ultimately to an instinctual urge to recreate this experience through procreation. The mature man desires innately to have a child, a relationship with whom will be based on the earliest infantile experiences of the prospective father's own life. His loving and nurturing nature is born from and rooted deeply in the earliest, primitive biological and psychological dependency on the love established within the bonding matrix of mother and infant. Emanating inherently from this mature, loving composition are the man's procreative aspirations and strivings. A man has with his mother a very intimate, personal, and long-standing identification; one that encourages his wish for a child. This child will be loved by him as he was loved by his mother.[3] Simultaneously, the man has formed with his father a gender based identification crystalizing his procreative ability and propensity to use it, wishing to produce a being as his father produced him. Both maternal and paternal identifications develop in an intertwined fashion from infancy to adulthood to formulate a meaning of, and purpose for, fathering a child. Fatherhood, then, is based on both feminine and masculine wishes to procreate and the opportunity to express both.[4] In fatherhood, these seemingly polarized ambitions take form as one.

Universal to all men is a desire, mostly in the unconscious realm of experience, to carry and give birth to a child. The man envies the woman's reproductive capacities and fantasizes about the production of a child from within his own body. In most cultures, however, this revelation would be vehemently denied since it contradicts the societal push for the acquisition and expression of innate "maleness" in gender identity. Indeed, there is an inherent biologically and psychologically predisposed drive for masculinity in the male sex. However, the male child does develop at conception from within the mother's womb and postnatally from the mother-infant matrix. The self of the young child in his individuated form extends in development from mother's relinquished desire for merger with her infant in facilitating favor of his age appropriate bid for autonomy and emancipation. Therefore, the young child, male or female, cannot help but to form a very strong personal identification with the mother and thus wish to be like her in all her wondrous ways including the capacity to produce and mother offspring. The young boy fantasizes about having a child of his own kind and of his own mother's making. This fantasy increasingly crystalizes through childhood, adolescence, and into young adulthood. While this wish, however, is normally repressed deep into the unconscious, there are many men who are nonetheless consciously aware of their feminine envy and are free to openly admit it. For them, it simply cannot be denied that women behold a unique and special power to create within their own bodies a child who will forever and unconditionally maintain an emotional attachment to them. A man's yearning for a child is founded on this acknowledgment and acceptance. This in turn stirs long-standing and unattainable reproductive wishes within his complex, unconscious mind.

While femininity is defined socially to include, and in fact is often high-lighted by, motherhood, masculinity can be defined by potency and virility. Masculinity expresses itself in the ultimate form of fatherhood and ideally in fatherliness. Modern American culture is heavily leaning in the direction of not only accepting but encouraging fatherly love, tenderness, and nurturance. The man receives gratification from the expression of his heterosexual love for his wife and solidifies his masculinity through conceiving with her a child in this love. While virility pronounces his masculine identity, it is an identity that is nonetheless threatened by the resurgence of acknowledged identification with his mother and the manifested envy of a woman's childbearing capacity. The young boy strives hard to individuate the self and establish a male gender identity. Under the guise of asserting his sexual prowess and proving his productive ability, the adult man defends against his unconscious fear of regressing to a state of infantile dependence on his mother. Conflict ensues for the man regarding conscious wishes for dependency and gratification of normal needs and wishes and the aspiration of his ego to prove his masculine independence, autonomy, and self-sufficiency. The polarized but simultaneous wishes for dependence and gratification and an equal desire for autonomy and sense of self present a normal struggle that all individuals face through their lifespan and never completely resolve.

This conflict is perhaps even more true of the male gender. The man's social and psychological role is that of capturing and preserving an active position in a progressive movement toward asserting his masculine strength and potency in his marriage, social life, and career. Yet there remain in every man inherent and unavoidable vulnerabilities, anxieties, and doubts. Infantile, yet normal, unconscious fantasies and wishes for regressive retreat into the loving symbiosis of mother and infant passively assimilating mother's loving provisions, persist to antagonize his conscious ego aspirations.

Nature provides a solution to the partly conscious conflict that ensues for the young man. The solution lies in the man's desire to procreate, to produce a child of his own kind. In doing so, he expresses his active stirrings through his sexual and psychological virility while simultaneously identifying with the natural passivity of his progeny nestled in mother's arms. This allays the conflict between concurrent desires for activity and passivity—to nurture and be nurtured. Prospective fatherhood promotes in the mature man a safe means of resolving the conflict of dependence versus independence while socially and psychologically adapting himself to the adult world of reality. The man proves that he can take care of himself as well as his wife and child, giving him a sense of purpose, meaning, and direction in life. He wishes to capture a sense of success in his manliness—success as defined by the modeled role of his own father. It is a young boy's fervent wish to achieve in equality what his father achieved through fathering him.[5] With the advent of mature manhood and genuine love for his wife and child, his wish may be actualized.

The man's desire for a child affords him the fantasy and potential to expand his emotional development and enrich his marriage as well as his sense of self. This is a healthy movement toward the maturity and consolidation of his personality, one inclusive of a paternal component in confluence with all other realms of his personal being. The mere thought of advancing to this higher level of personality through the mystique of fatherhood is enticing. The mature man in desire of a child reflects on his relationship to his father, past and present—a father with whom the man has identified intensely. This is primarily an identification with the goodliness of his father's fatherliness. He may also fantasize about how he might father his own child by his own merit. These fantasies provide for the actualization of the goodliness of his own fathering efforts. A man's wish for a child provides him with the hope of recapturing the healthy aspects of his relationship with his father while simultaneously reworking the normally ungratifying aspects of that relationship. Thus, in fathering his own child, a man anticipates the opportunity to vicariously undo the internally sustained conflicts of his own childhood experiences and empathizes with his child by re-experiencing what it was like in search of the "good" father. The man believes that he can enrich and solidify the relationship with his father by becoming a father just like his father has been and by producing a child (grandchild) for him. What a man believes a good father should be like becomes the ideal for which he strives and presents to his own father. From the man's point of view, he and his father have "teamed up" in the context of their father-son relationship to, in effect, create a third generation child. The man's identification with his own father in combination with his own established fathering ideal culminates in that which he anticipates and desires his own fatherliness to be like. This gives the prospective father delight, ambition, and hope.

It is not only the father to which the man wishes to present his own child as a gift. He desires to give this same gift to his mother, wishing to give to his mother a life just as she had given life to him a generation before. This gift of a child is a being of both his and his mother's own kind. Thus the man wishes to produce with his wife a child out of his genuine love for the woman of his choice and because his wife represents to a vicariously significant degree, albeit of unconscious awareness, the equivalent of the man's mother.

The gift of the child takes on yet another dimension for the man. Enraptured by the bliss of their love, the wife and husband conceive their child, bringing them closer in unification. Acknowledgment of his wife's pregnancy as a gift of love from her to him bringing him to a joy so impenetrable that he becomes completely absorbed in the experience of his manliness and all that it entails, the man acknowledges and accepts his new responsibility and commitment. As anticipated, the prospect of fatherhood does present itself as a challenge for the excited yet anxious person that he is. But what the man may not anticipate is that the reality of impending fatherhood and the emotional upheaval that it stirs from within will be experienced as a crisis.[6] Just as conception and pregnancy is a critical event of profound psychological significance for the woman, so, too, is prospective fatherhood for the man having to adapt if he is to maintain his psychological equilibrium. But once the reality of his pending fatherhood is recognized, the husband comes to accept with poise and courage his new paternal identity and role, and may become proud of his new self-image of "family man." He assumes with dignity the role of sheltering and nurturing his beloved wife and their soon-to-be child. His self-esteem is heightened with a sense of power in proclamation of his sexual potency. But of even more significance is the exuberance and grandiosity the man feels at having initiated what may prove to be the most meaningful and purposeful event of his life—nurturing his unborn child in spite of his anxieties. This is what it means to be a man.

The loving bond between the man and his pregnant wife intensifies for the husband. Not only is their mutual love solidified symbolically and practically by the growing fetus of their own creation but also, for the man, his wife's pregnancy links him to his beloved mother with whom he identifies increasingly.[7] The husband and father-to-be imbues both his wife and mother with qualities that represent in his eyes nothing less than the ultimate of wondrous beauty and power. The wife radiates with a brilliance outweighed only by the ascending potency of the husband. At the same time, however, it behooves him to surrender himself to her endowment—the uniquely feminine capacity to bear a child. In the midst of his elation, the loving husband is, nonetheless, the epitome of humility. The man places himself in secondary significance to his wife. While this resignation may prove to be difficult, it holds potential for fostering his emotional maturity. This event should validate the husband's sense of manliness rather than threaten it. It is also in this state of affairs that part of the prospective father's ego regresses to an earlier stage of childhood development wherein he surrenders to the inherent and undeniable dependence on his mother, relinquishing his perceived omnipotence and identifying the underdeveloped, fragile self with the more powerful yet loving mother.

The man forms a new and more mature identification with his own mother in her altruistic maternal role.

His wife's pregnancy is a time of emotional turbulence for the prospective father. He is inspired by hopes and anticipations of the child's development, yet fears for the child's physical and psychological well-being. Also, the enhanced nurturing abilities of the mother are both admired and envied by the husband, potentially drawing him either closer to or further away from his wife. The wife's normal preoccupation with the fetus growing inside of her leaves the husband feeling to some degree displaced or rejected. Ideally, however, the husband will come to identify with her nurturing activities which, in turn, will establish the foundation on which he will prepare for his own nurturing and caretaking duties. This will allow him to face the arousal of his own feminine wishes for childbearing and other maternal functions and integrate them into the maleness of his personality by becoming the ideal father figure. The feminine wishes that cannot be actualized because of his biological makeup can be compensated for by maintaining and enhancing the loving relationship with his wife. In addition, he can be available physically and emotionally to meet his wife's needs. This is an opportune time for both prospective parents to share their feelings and fantasies concerning their unborn child, the birthing experience, and postpartum care so that they may form a cooperative and supportive alliance in their impending parenthood. A mutual effort is made to become more functionally interdependent. In addition to his envy of the pregnant wife, the husband experiences immense gratitude for her blessing of pregnancy. He idealizes her, which is precisely what the pregnant woman needs to help ease her own anxieties and bolster her self-esteem and confidence. In return, he feels that he is serving as provider and protector of his family. Through this, he prepares himself for the ensuing father-infant relationship.

The strong relationship that the man experiences with his wife remains through parturition. The father, at the moment of birth, wants reassurance above all else that his wife's condition is sound and secure. In fact, it is the man's response to his wife's expanding needs and vacillating emotions during pregnancy that formally usher in the initial relationship between the father and his newborn child. In a short time, the father expands his concern for his wife's well-being to include the welfare of his child. While the father remains at the periphery through his wife's pregnancy, distance between father and child is immediately obliterated when he is presented face to face with the very flesh of his creation. A highly emotionally charged relationship is established and the father-to-infant bond emerges. This moment is the peak of the maturational line of manhood.

At the point of inception of an altruistic love for his infant, the father is governed by a strong sense of hope an aspiration. The father's wish is threefold in nature: He aspires for the happy, healthy development of his beloved child; he envisions a future of a loving, emotional attachment forever held; and he prepares himself for the unfolding of an increasingly enriched and affirmed sense of a self in his fathering experience. The stage is set as the newborn gazes into the eyes of what will be increasingly perceived as the embodiment of strength and wisdom—its loving and beloved father. Mutual gaze and reciprocal cooing cannot help but to encourage the flow of tenderness from the loving empathic father, which in turn activates his own maternal strivings. Ongoing childhood memories of having been soothed, contained, and nurtured by his mother solidify his innate motherliness. Equally important, the fatherliness that was provided him by his own father directs the means by which he interacts emotionally with his infant. The loving father is modeled by one's own loving father.[8]

Although memories of the good mother and father along with their identifications heighten the father's confidence in his effectively fathering his own infant, the fathering ideal overshadows the importance of his mother. The man does not, however, completely relinquish his identification with his mother but, rather, transfers the maternal ideal to his wife who enacts the maternal aspects in relation to their newborn. The father thereby experiences great pleasure witnessing his wife's joy and delight in their child. The mother-infant relationship is an added source of love for the father, who, in identification with his father, assumes with dignity his role as facilitator and protector of that dyad. This also enhances his loving relationships with his wife and child individually. In particular, the father's relationship to his newborn is generated by two subjectively potent experiences: He identifies with the infant itself and therefore exhibits genuine empathy and concern for his loved one; he also identifies with his own father, which gives him awareness of how to raise a child and what it means to be a father. In identification with his own father, and because he endears his child, the father desires and seeks to attain the image of the good father. This image, as has been mentioned, is derived partly from memories of being fathered in his own childhood. In addition, the good father is an image derived from fantasy that has developed and flourished through his life. The fantasized image is of that which the maturing child, adolescent, and young adult sees as the perfect father. Just as the woman establishes a "maternal ideal," so, too, does the man establish a "paternal ideal"—that which serves as the paternal position a man adopts in his fathering duties.[9] The image of the real father with whom the man identifies in interaction with the image of the personally derived paternal ideal serves as the prototype of the father that the man will become to his child. He sorts out those fathering experiences of his childhood and the paternal aspects of his own father that he believes will benefit him in fathering his own child, and integrates them into those aspects of the self that he believes will appropriately fit his personality as it is to be expressed in his fathering duties. With this dualistic picture of the good father, he forges his ascendancy into fatherhood.

The father-infant relationship is proclaimed the instant the father holds in his arms the very flesh of his offspring and makes eye to eye contact. The emotional intensity of this experience for the father is of unquestionably profound significance to their relationship. However, for the infant in the prime of its life, this experience is qualitatively different from that afforded by the envelopment of mother's loving arms. Mutual gesture and response between mother and infant is instinctual and intuitive in nature for both the mother and newborn. The two are primed for a bond that is innate to their biological makeup and that cannot be supplanted by substituting the father for the mother. Nevertheless, the presence of the father in all his desire and hope is of deep-seated and encompassing influence on the mother-infant relationship. Although the father may not be finely tuned to the cues and gestures his infant uses to signal its needs and wishes, he is keenly attuned to the intricacies of his wife's engagement with their infant. The intuitive father recognizes the predisposition of his wife and infant to uniquely fit one another in relationship. He accepts this natural phenomenon and acquires gratification not only in witnessing its evolution but also in acknowledging that it actually appeals to a sensitively integral part of his very self.

The mother, transversely, is empathically in tune to her husband's wish for involvement in the dyadic relationship. Not only is she unselfish in her service to her beloved infant, but out of love for her husband she derives pleasure from periodically drawing him into the harmonious union. She serves as the catalyst to the developing emotional attachment between infant and father.[10] She utilizes the ease with which she and her newborn meld in relational interplay to smoothly and judiciously delegate some of her caretaking and loving functions to her husband. The father enthusiastically undertakes not only the "fun" aspects of parenthood but the practical aspects as well, and is elated when he is able to calm the child when the mother cannot. If the newborn is bottle fed, the father boasts with pride in acknowledgment that he has the capacity to nourish his child. If he can feed his beloved infant with food, then he can, in a more encompassing mode, provide for his totally dependent progeny. The father, too, is a source of generosity and love, and the infant soon senses this, again bolstering the man's self-confidence. Any father can attest to the unbridling sense of potency he feels while holding his newborn in the palms of his hands. The sheer strength of his manliness unleashes, yet so very gently, as does the all encompassing surgence of power and spirit that tantalizes and electrifies the experience of his being. This is a being that in its very essence is transfused into the being of his progeny. This is what the father has to offer his infant child—his manhood. And this can be accomplished by means nothing less than of indomitable love.

It is paradoxical that the masculinity of the father activates and promotes his motherliness. The father's desire to gently nurture his beloved infant is captured by the strength and virility he feels in his identity of manhood and fatherhood. His investment in serving as the protector of his family and the power with which this tendency manifests seems to melt, though actually strengthens, as his infant looks at him, coos at him, smiles at him, and reaches out to grasp him. This awakens the tenderness that often lies dormant within the man and activates the pleasurable memory traces of his own early experience in a loving, intimate relationship with his mother. These memory traces are at the core of the man's gentle and tender feelings toward his wife and their child, and they constitute the feminine component of his masculine identity. Fathering his infant-child in a motherly manner may seem to be a more safe and secure context in which the man feels comfortable in actualizing his feminine qualities. If this event is achieved, all three persons reap the rewards. Not only is this manner becoming increasingly socially acceptable, but a redeeming quality.

The man integrates his motherliness into his fatherliness to secure a firm identity in his fatherhood. This is a father who need not relinquish or deny his intimate and tender feelings in order to pronounce his role in service of guardianship to his family. He maintains this integrated position as he proceeds with the fathering experience. The father presents himself to his infant as the other object of its attention, affection, and desire, and the child relates to the father with love in gratitude for his pleasurable provisions.

Chapter Five

Love and Individuation: Differentiation and Integration in Toddlerhood

By the time an infant has reached the eighth month of life he or she has established a functional awareness outside his or her own being that a single source provides for its needs and wishes. The diffuse sense of separateness felt by the infant on the brink of toddlerhood coincides with the similarly diffuse sense of self emerging from the maturing child. A mother is increasingly perceived by her baby in the pre-stages of toddlerhood as not only the source of love and provisions, but also, as the one who holds potential for withholding these gratifying supplies. A baby acutely acknowledges that its wish for the beloved mother can be, and inherently often is, a wish that is frustrated. At this point of development, the instinctual urge and drive for the mother's love and intimation evolves into a qualitatively higher form of desire and petition for the same. The early toddler longs for the intimacy of mother's love while he or she develops an increasing sense of separateness from her. The view that mother is the one and only true love object crystalizes within the child's conceptual framework, becoming a significant maturational achievement not only for the early toddler, but also for the mother in her facilitating role.[1]

A developmental process is about to begin and lasts until the child reaches approximately thirty-six months of age. Psychoanalysis refers to this process as that of "separation - individuation."[2] What results is the child of three years experiencing and manifesting himself or herself as a progressively self-sufficient, autonomous person, while still requiring loving parental support. The three-year-old's age appropriate bid for autonomy and assertion highlights his ability to perceive, conceptualize, memorize, and test his surroundings, acting on his own volition and faculties. As the toddler differentiates from the mother, he gradually learns to integrate the new discoveries of his burgeoning self and expanded environment into a sense of identity. The toddler's identity is born from the mother-child attachment, yet develops parallel to the perceived, unfolding identity of his beloved mother. At the end of toddlerhood, the child can tenuously conceptualize in his mind that " I am Johnny, and I am three years old today. Over there is my mommy. I love her and she loves me. She has her own interests, needs, desires, and feelings distinct from my own. And even though there is space and distance between us, we share a loving, intimate attachment."

Tenuous as it proves to be for both the toddler and the mother, individuation is a process that occurs only within the facilitating atmosphere sustained by the caring and generous mother. She appropriately permits her child to take part in the creation of both his individuated self and its surroundings.

At the age of eight months, an infant is no longer perfectly contented to be snuggled lovingly in its mother's enveloping arms. The early toddler acquires an increasing sensory acuity and responsivity to surrounding stimuli. He sees, hears, smells, tastes, and tactically feels things with strengthening precision and heightened interest. Likewise, the early toddler acquires the ability to move and position his body in interface with the sources of his new stimulation. The child's perceptual capacity allows him to distinguish the bodily self from the body of his mother. The early toddler can now visually scan his mother's body with delight and fascination, and learn that there is more to his mother than her inviting face and nourishing breast.[3] The child on the brink of toddlerhood strokes his mother's body, pulls on her hair, grabs her cheeks, and pokes his fingers in her eyes and mouth. He can also listen more attentively to his mother's voice and marvel in the smell of her perfume and bodily aromas. The early toddler may be entranced with mother's attire, especially the colorful and shiny objects such as watches and eyeglasses. The mother is comprised of many delightful characteristics previously unfamiliarized. These characteristics become highly invested with love.

Soon the young toddler acquires the motor capacity to wiggle away from mother's lap in attempt to attain a broader view and scope the entirety of mother and what she is all about. Sitting on the floor at her feet, the child sees mother in her totality, witnessing and experiencing whatever else she has to offer with her presence. Motivated by her timely encouragement, the toddler with great effort and determination learns to crawl away from his mother. Pursuing with fascination the outside world, he begins to allow for spatial distance between himself and his mother. The early toddler believes that he has created, by his own power, a space which constitutes his new world, and takes pride in this creation.[4] Physically distanced from the mother, the child can obtain not only a vastly new perspective on his self-made world, but also a pragmatically new view of his mother. This in turn furthers the toddler's delight in his expanding faculties and increases his loving investment in the good mother, a mother that he himself designs. The intuitive mother promotes her child's illusion that he is the creator of his expanding world and shares in his excitement.

The mother remains in close proximity to her adventurous toddler so he may readily return at his discretion. Each time the toddler crawls back to mother from short explorations, he illusively believes that he in actuality rediscovers her, as if she had temporarily disappeared. And each return qualitatively alters the perception he has of his mother and increases affection for her. Physically distanced from the mother, the child is enchanted with his ability to recognize, observe, and admire her from afar. With each new venture away from and in return to the available mother, the loving relationship between the toddler and his mother assumes a new and progressive quality. This is a quality that the empathically sensitive mother allows her child to create and recreate in delightful anticipation and hope for both.

The mother physically and emotionally positions herself as the center of her toddler's expanding world, a home base to which the child can return to confirm his continued attachment to her. This transpires despite her child's belief that he is the hub of his self-created universe. The adventurous early toddler invests love and adoration in his repeatedly newfound self, a self in loving relation to his repeatedly newfound mother. Mother exaltedly takes pride in her facilitation of this inspirational achievement.

Perhaps the single most monumental step towards individuation is when the toddler learns to stand and begins to walk, actively moving away from his mother, and capable of coming and going more or less at his own discretion. This achievement is, once again, from the child's perspective, of his own creation. Wondrous as it is, walking seems to come naturally for the toddler who does not question its acquisition, but rather relishes its effects. The child is capable of readily moving toward or away from his mother, approaching new objects of his environment, and maneuvering his body to view things from differing positions. This is a celebrated conquest for the toddler who is now in total exhilaration. The environment is now available to explore, manipulate, and master. The toddler feels omnipotent in regard to his newly acquired motor ability, opening the door for endless engagement with a strange but appealing world. With a quest for life, the elated toddler aims to expand his love beyond that for the mother to include his new acquisition—the self in relation to the seemingly infinite universe. Temporarily oblivious to mother's presence or absence, the early toddler pursues his objective to incorporate the vast world of the yet-to-be known. The toddler is seemingly indifferent to mother's whereabouts due to a perceived sense of omnipotence. He still thinks of his mother as an extension of himself. "Wherever I go, there goes mother as well." The mother is taken for granted as being there to energize and protect. However, the toddler in his drive for conquest does not yet realize that he is subject to inevitable experiences of powerlessness, helplessness, and vulnerability. Having attained safety and security in the enveloping arms of the mother as an infant, the adventurous child now seeks the same solace in a different modality, by the magical incorporation of the powerfully expansive universe into his own sense of self.

A mother faces the difficult task of accepting her toddler's age appropriate bid for individuation. She painfully bears the loss of her child's previous dependence on her. An empathic mother ironically experiences the pain simultaneous to the joy she shares in identification with her toddler's maturation. She knows that she is the facilitating source of this maturation inspite of her toddler's triumphant belief that he has originated his own achievement. It is the truly loving mother who encourages and teaches her toddler to walk. And this paradox is not an expression of the mother's ambivalence concerning her loved one's independence. Rather it exemplifies the acknowledgment and acceptance of her child's need for support and encouragement as he partakes in his quest for autonomy. In teaching her toddler to walk, the mother holds out her arms as if to balance him. Indeed, the toddler may illusively believe that he is being physically supported by his mother's merely outstretched arms, while actually performing on his own. The toddler is motivated by his mother's encouraging smile and praise that beckons him to walk into the security of her awaiting, enveloping arms. The mother's love, therefore, serves as the inspiration for learning how to walk—the walk towards individuation.

As the child ventures away from his mother he vicariously takes her along. The toddler carries the mother through his own sense of omnipotence, as if the exploring toddler inherently knows that mother is there to support him all the way. The world that the toddler discovers as beyond himself and his mother is imbued with maternal attributes and he invests himself in this maternally protective world.[5] The toddler's world, in effect, is just like his mother—exciting, fascinating, and inviting, and he wishes to share it with his mother, filling the psychological gap created by his separations. When the toddler returns from his brief expeditions he will bring to her specifically chosen items such as a shoe, a book, or a rock acquired along the way. The child may deposit these items in his mother's lap as a place of refuge that the toddler himself is not quite ready to relinquish. He shares delight with mother by offering her a gift of his own creation. This gift serves as a token of appreciation and enduring love.[6]

Assured that the precious belongings are safe and secure in his mother's presence, the toddler prepares for his next venture. Nonetheless, there are times when he chooses to remain with his mother, inviting her to share in the fond treasures of his exploration, which rekindles the emotional attachment they both wish to preserve. The loving bond between the adventurous toddler and his encouraging and supporting mother permits and impels the child to utilize the mother as a perceived extension of his own self. This allows the yet fragile self to maintain an illusion of merger with her; a mother who, from the child's perspective, is there with and as a part of the toddler to support him in pursuit of individuation. However, because the toddler shares his feats and newly created worldly acquisitions with his mother, he nonetheless securely permits himself to experience mother as an increasingly separate being. She is the *person* who receives her child's gifts. And he maintains connection to her through the sharing experience. The empathic mother promotes her beloved toddler's vacillation between the illusion of merger and the reality sense of his increasing separation from her.

As the child's sense of distinction between himself and his mother develops, he increasingly acknowledges his inherent dependence on her and begins to fear their previously desired union. The toddler feels overwhelmed by her power and fears the possibility of ceasing to exist as a being of his own. The anxiety producing fantasy is augmented by the acknowledgment of his increasing autonomy, a self-sufficiency otherwise relished by the aspiring toddler. His autonomy is now threatened by his own insecurity about facing the world independently, and paradoxically, he becomes aware of his dependence on his mother's support in facilitating and upholding his independence.

In order to defend against the overwhelming experience, the toddler may feel a greater need to assert and proclaim his powers. The sense of omnipotence intensifies as a defense against his own increasing sense of vulnerability. He establishes an illusion of self-sufficiency. However, with a concomitant strengthening of reality testing, the toddler cannot avoid being aware of his inherent weakness in interaction with the increasingly complex and frustrating environment. Previously feeling good about himself in his successful influence with the environment, the toddler may begin to feel assailable and his self-esteem lowers—a very painful experience.[7]

In the normal developmental process, the toddler compensates for the perceived sense of weakness and self-doubt by developing fantasies of grandeur in a desperate attempt to reestablish the faltering sense of cohesion. Frightened and angry about his dependence on the mother, the toddler may build resistance to her invasion of his tenaciously clung-to domain, marking his territory, physically and emotionally, excluding the mother at will. The toddler into his third year of life asserts his autonomy by learning to say "no," and develops a sense of entitlement by saying "mine." It is indeed a trying task for a mother to empathize with and respect her child's defensive need to pronounce himself in the form of aggression.

The mother's empathic availability permits her toddler to lessen his defensive stature in maintaining his self-regard and self-cohesion. The fantasies of grandeur mentioned earlier are normal and necessary though they delay his capacity to test reality. The empathic and loving mother takes it upon herself to soften the onslaughts experienced by her child at the hands of the real world of knocks and blows to both his physical and emotional being. The toddler begins to see the world as no longer all his own. The mother partially shields her child's increasing awareness of his inadequacies and inferiority. She reconstructs in her toddler's fragile self-experience that which is repeatedly knocked down by the adversities and afflictions of daily living. She does this by praising her toddler and genuinely admiring him for every achievement made. As her child acquires new conceptual and physical capabilities, such as learning new words, the ability to run and jump, to use the toilet, and feed himself, the loving mother is there to praise and diffuse her child's self-doubt. Indeed, it is not surprising or harmful for the mother to go overboard and "make a big deal" of what may seem trite to the casual observer. The maintenance of the child's self-esteem is contingent on both his actual accomplishments and his mother's consistent praise and loving admiration. The mother who affirms her beloved toddler teaches her child to affirm himself.

At this critical point in his life, the child of toddlerhood needs to declare himself and be affirmed in this declaration. As the mother facilitates this, her child acquires a growing awareness of not only his personal strengths and weaknesses, but equally importantly, the feeling states engendered by this awareness. Likewise, the toddler, too, can empathize with the mother, and does so, not only out of love and appreciation for her, but also out of his acknowledged need to maintain a connection to her. The toddler who has faith in his mother's capability and willingness to provide the nutriment and aliment he requires to sustain his well-being, also acquires self-assurance in regard to his ability to justly elicit these loving ministrations. In essence, the toddler perceives himself as being a worthy and lovable person. As he gradually expands in autonomy and self-sufficiency, the child internalizes what is now seen as the mother's omnipotence and grandeur previously thought to be his own. The internalization of mother's competency and strength sustains the toddler's self-esteem and overall well-being as the two partners in unity sever their ties step by step in compliance with nature's eventual plan for the toddler's emancipation and individuation.

Individuation is a long, arduous process for the toddler. He relinquishes his infantile sense of merger with his mother, painfully experiences the downfall of his sense of omnipotence and grandiosity, and humbly surrenders to the reality of his mother's power and influence over him. This occurs, nonetheless, under the positive valence of mutual love between the mother and child. Eventually, the toddler acquires a more realistic view of himself, one that illuminates his dependency on the mother as well as a more mature and realistic view of her. Empathizing with the mother's needs and feelings, the toddler engages a higher quality relationship with her. Identifying with his mother's effectiveness in dealing with a sometimes overwhelming world, the ambitious child is free to venture away from mother to strengthen his own skills in confrontation with the complexities and perplexities of life. Because the mother loves and supports her individuating child, the toddler feels lovable and worthy of mother's guidance and support. By internalizing and identifying with the mother's strength and competency, the child develops a love for the self balancing his love for the mother.

The mother progressively lets go of her individuating toddler, as the child self-assuredly ventures out to assimilate and accommodate more and more of his environment. Self-confidence is founded on the omnipotence he attributes realistically to his mother and carries with him as aliment to his own eager strivings. He returns to his mother periodically to secure her support and comfort as well as to confirm her continued presence.

A toddler is equally captivated by mother's own activities of exploration, guided by her own interests and wishes. Following the mother about closely, the toddler inquisitively observes her every action. Mother is afforded the opportunity to share the products of her explorations, as does her child with her. A simple routine activity such as doing the laundry can thoroughly entrance the child in observing his mother's seemingly magical abilities. The mother may solicit her toddler's involvement and assistance, highlighting and crystallizing the sharing experience, enhancing their partnership.

A mother's willingness to periodically share her own experiences with her loved one is crucial. It balances the increasingly longer periods of time in which the toddler is away from her. The child's maturing cognitive faculties permit him to engage in even more complex actions with his expanding world, and he becomes acutely aware of his body and its functions, encouraging even further exploration. Locomotor capabilities, such as running and climbing, allow the toddler to traverse more territory and venture further from mother's presence. Now it takes a longer time to return to the mother often out of hearing range. Should an incident occur away from the mother's protective purview, such as a topple down the staircase, the pain of defeat solidifies the toddler's awareness that indeed he is a distinct, separate being from the mother. The mother's omnipotence no longer serves aliment to his sense of self. The toddler must face the world on his own terms. It is at this time, also, that the child begins to experience a greater variety of emotions, such as sadness, fear and elation. These are feelings that he cannot yet differentiate from one another or integrate effectively into his self-experience. Feelings about his mother are perplexing to the toddler, and he may begin to feel both positive and negative emotions about her, accentuating the already marked ambivalence in his polarized wishes to be both with and separate from the mother. This creates anxiety for the child. His cognitive faculties are sufficiently strong to fundamentally conceptualize, by the age of approximately twenty months, that he is indeed a separate and distinct being, and one that can no longer share in mother's strength and competency. Yet the toddler is acutely aware at both an intellectual and emotional level that he needs his mother. More specifically, he needs his mother's love.

Fearing that both the mother and her love will abandon him, the toddler nearing the end of his second year follows her about incessantly and clings to her out of desperation. Mothers are often perplexed as to why their toddler of about twenty months who thoroughly enjoyed emancipation just a month or two earlier is now holding tenaciously to her presence and reassurance. The troubled toddler repeatedly woos the mother, enticing her into repetitive demonstrations of her enduring love. Ceasing to venture far from mother, the anxious child checks regularly on his mother's whereabouts and takes every opportunity to attempt to engage her in his exploits. The sensitive mother, despite concern and frustration, responds to her loved one's fear with as much consistency as possible, reassuring her child that neither she nor her love will cease. This dramatic situation, the crisis of individuation, typically subsides by the time the toddler reaches his second birthday.[8]

The toddler does, nonetheless, continue to experience some separation anxiety in mother's absence. Because the child of twenty-four months is almost fully aware of his separateness from mother and is completely aware of his dependence on her for his continued sense of well-being, he experiences a sharp and discerning sense of loss without her presence. The child wants and needs his mother, and can only be assured when his mother is physically and emotionally attentive. The loss the toddler experiences results not only in separation anxiety, but also in a state of mourning.

In the child's third year of life, bouts of separation anxiety and saddened mood persist. However, the toddler steadily becomes emotionally equipped to tolerate disappointment and frustration at the hands of his disengaging and increasingly unavailable mother. By internalizing the mother's active provisions of love, support, and nurturance, the child acquires the ability to tolerate anxiety and sadness, control tension, and ultimately to sooth himself and advance his sense of trust and credence in himself. Increasingly self-reliant, the child in his third year of life relinquishes the magical illusion of the perfectly responsive mother in favor of the newly acquired capacity to be his uniquely own person.

As the child experiences anxiety and sadness when physically disengaged from his mother, he readily evokes within his mind the image of his mother and the image of the self in relationship with her.[9] The toddler conceptualizes that "yes, mother still does exist, as does myself in loving relation to her." This, in and of itself, sufficiently comforts the toddler for increasingly longer periods of time, until mother once again is physically available. The internal images, or representations, of the mother, the self, and the mutually gratifying relationship between the two comprise a self-regulating internal world promoting the toddler's ability to perform those functions previously provided by the mother, principally within the realm of her soothing services. This internal-world entity is referred to in psychoanalysis in broad definition as the "ego." The ego is an integral component of the overall self that permits the toddler to meet some of his own physical and emotional needs with increasingly minimal dependence on the mother.

The child's self-regulating and self-sustaining ego functions now permit him to experience maternal soothing as emanating from within, enhancing confirmation, affirmation, and esteem as the toddler becomes more integrated as a whole person and facilitates both the capacity and propensity to consolidate his expanding spectrum of emotions. The toddler becomes one who has good, loving feelings toward his mother in all her goodliness, and bad, frustrating feelings toward his mother in her inability to tend to her loved one's every need and wish. By the end of toddlerhood, the child acquires the cognitive ability to recognize that it is the same mother who both frustrates and gratifies him. He concomitantly understands that he is the same person who at times feels frustrated and angry with the mother and at other times feels unalloyed devotion to and admiration of her. The good and bad images of the mother blend as do the good and bad images of himself, coalescing into an equally whole, integrated, and cohesive sense of personhood. The child loves both himself and his mother even when he is frustrated in their relationship. Likewise the child recognizes that his mother still loves him even when he is frustrated with her. His sense of self also maintains continuity as he acknowledges that he is the same loving and lovable person today that he was yesterday and that he is the same loving and lovable person when with his mother as when he is alone. As well, the child understands that he is the same loving and lovable person when he is feeling sad as when feeling happy.

Now that the child of three years acquires an integrated sense of the self as an individuated and substantially more, though not yet fully, autonomous person, he comes to realize that he has both a place in and influence on his world inclusive of his mother. The child develops concern for his mother's feelings and how his feelings influence her. With the increased capacity for empathy, his sense of self takes on new meaning and purpose, and his expanding social and object world centers now around the core of his "feeling" self. Love, intimacy, and relational attachment advance to a higher, more sophisticated and matured level of experience for both the mother and child. At the close of toddlerhood, the mother may delight in her child's display of a uniquely pronounced personality—a person of his own being, sensitive and generous.

This is the mother's very creation, and she, too, should be proud.

Chapter Six

Love and the Family Triangle

The individuated child of three years recognizes himself as a distinct person. Additionally, he acknowledges he is a person very much like his beloved mother. Having experienced his mother's love in so many ways, he now understands that he returns his love to her in many ways, bringing him great delight. The child strengthens his newly established identification with his mother in the realization that both he and his mother are equally loving and lovable persons. Additionally, the child recognizes both himself and his mother as persons with feelings, and these emotions germinate a reciprocal flow of affection, heightening the young child's sense of separateness. He can clearly determine the boundaries between himself and others, an achievement that inaugurates the formation of an identity. Yet, this maturational milestone illuminates the anxiety producing fact of his still pliable and vulnerable state of being.

Striving intently to strengthen and secure his self-defining boundaries, the child again looks to those whose assistance he has already relied on. Initially, it is mother, and secondarily, father. Yet, he struggles to hold claim to the individual personhood he has crafted for himself by mobilizing age appropriate assertion and aggression. He commands his separateness and punctuates his independence, strengthening his boundaries and the cohesiveness of his own self.

Yet, the three-year-old yearns for mother's emotional replenishment. His personal esteem and value as a loving and lovable person is contingent on her continued availability in intimate connection. The young child wants mother to respond to his every action to ensure his worthiness as a person, and one deserving of his mother's love. As discussed in chapter five, although the child alternates between dependence and independence, there remains an age appropriate bid for both the girl and the boy, though more pronounced for the boy, to disengage from the mother-child dyad.

The advancement of the child's emotional skills include the ability to perceive one's own emotions as well as those of significant others, especially his mother's, and the sensibility of the mutuality and reciprocal nature of their relationship. Additionally, the child's growing cognitive faculties permit him to conceptualize that he influences, and is influenced by, things and events in his external environment. Motor functions such as running, jumping, and wrestling along with increased endurance and strength beckon the child. Psychomotor acuity allows the child to predict with forethought how his actions can influence and direct the outcome of an event, mastering the concept of cause and effect.[1]

Psychomotor abilities also provide the child with the mastery skills that improve his self-functioning and provide him with personal esteem needed for his expanding world. Father, siblings, grandparents, neighbors, preschool friends and teachers encourage the child to experiment with social interplay.

Disengaging from the primal mother-infant bond and relinquishing its tranquility is a precarious and anxiety filled process. The child takes special care not to defy, decry, or disavow the primary relationship he and his mother have so intuitively created. Yet, the child necessarily disengages his mother while simultaneously disidentifying with her, relying on substitute identifications that take the form of his own functional capacities. He incorporates his mother and her goodliness into his own personality structure and developing repertoire of self-functions. In effect, as the child disengages his mother he simultaneously develops and utilizes an internal image of her. The self and the maternal image coordinate and efficiently serve the child's needs, increasingly identifying with his own capabilities and achievements.

The young child is painfully reluctant to let go of his beloved mother. He does so as a matter of natural course, tenaciously clinging for security to his internalized image of her as he traverses the path to the social world of other intriguing and soon-to-be significant persons in his life. The heightened ambivalence the child has for his mother induces periodic aggressiveness towards her as a desperate means of punctuating his independence. He is aided in his dilemma by the persona of another crucial figure in his life: His father.

During infancy the father is just as much a source of inquisitiveness to the infant as his child is to him. The father during infancy is that mysteriously delightful figure in the background who remains on the periphery of the mother-infant dyad, while yet offering a beckoning call. The father is there when his infant is in want of other-than-mother attention.[2] During toddlerhood, the father is not only available, but actually alluring, exciting, and different than the mother. The father is the being who sometimes quietly, sometimes loudly, sometimes gently, and sometimes harshly, engages the child. Father is perceived by his child as a strong yet peripheral person not yet at the toddler's unqualified disposal.

As the three-year-old disengages his mother, the father's position assumes a more definitive and purposeful role as one who becomes the very source of excitement. The child is challenged and electrified by the father and this is equally true for both girls and boys, and not qualitatively different for the two genders. The loving father both roughhouses and gently caresses his child regardless of gender.

His inevitably perceived sense of helplessness confirms the child's belief that mother and father are the all-knowing, all-strong, perfect caretakers of his sustenance. He lovingly idealizes his parents and ascribes to them the omnipotence that he will, in time, take into himself. In optimal doses, the child alternates his attention to each parent, determining for himself the degree to which he relies on one or the other, or both.

While the parents serve a vital function, the mother and father are not perceived as a single functioning unit working in concert. Rather, each parent is perceived uniquely with differing characteristics and furnishings, and ascribed differing roles, functions, and purposes. The child will forever consider the mother to be the primary figure who provides for the secure and sustained relationship. The father is the prospective vehicle in which to traverse the path to eventual self-sufficiency and independence.

Ever so cautiously the young child approaches the mysteriously presented and grandly received father and creates for himself a perfect, new relationship with him. The three-year-old child is not quite sure where this guy comes from, but the father is certainly exciting and tempting, and the child knows that father loves him as does his mother. Moreover, the child specifically feels a strong love for his father. In spite of his ambivalence, the young child realizes that there is a great big world out there, in which he must find his viable place. The mother is the facilitator of the special task oriented relationship between the father and child, and the child is gratefully aware of the mother's generous deference and approval.

With a facilitating family environment, the child is prepared to pursue autonomy by attributing different functions to each parent, and struggling to maintain a balance between the desire to merge with his mother and the push to become a distinct person in his own right.

The child alternates between his two parents in soliciting needed services, securing, for example, affirmation of his maturing personhood from the mother who shows absolute astonishment with his every accomplishment. The mother idealizes her loved one, reflecting her delight as she inspires her child to idealize and love himself in his worthiness. The father, in turn, may serve as the calling light by which his child frees himself to explore and engage his social and physical world. Mother is a safe container providing security, confirmation, and limit-setting while father opens the door to the testing of newly developing social, cognitive, and motor skills. Mother helps her child attenuate the frustration he inevitably experiences at the hands of a perplexing and challenging world. The child needs to encounter this frustration in moderation and in optimal doses as a successful means of truly testing himself and learning, hands-on, what talents and shortcomings he inherently possesses.

The child learns lessons of love and intimation from the mother and tenderness and sensitivity from the father in the context of trust, concern, empathy, and love created by both parents. The child creates two special relationships with his parents. But with expanding cognitive abilities and social awareness, he sharply recognizes that he is not the only one who partakes in the loving intimate relations. Indeed, other significant persons in the child's life can and do pursue relationships with one another, excluding him. This awareness that his newly created social circle does not center around himself is striking. Another maturational milestone is reached, but the youngster finds himself in a bit of a quandary.

The child of three years has a basic understanding that his mother and father have a special relationship comprised of and defined by themselves. The parents are no longer viewed by the child as personal extensions in his service. And to heighten the intensity, the mother and father love one another as much as they love their child, and as much as he loves them. The child conceptualizes this as he conceives all newly discovered elements of his social and physical world. He believes, by means of fantasy, that he created this occurrence and for his own utility. Yet, the powerful implication of this creation presents the child with a dilemma—his mother and father loving one another in a way that excludes him. The discovery shocks the illusion that the child is at the core of not only his own existence, but the existence of the universe as he knows it.

The nature of the love between mother and father is identified by the child as being of the same type and quality as he experiences with each. He believes that he transfers his personally enjoyed experiences of intimation with mother and father to the arena of the parental pair. In his view, the love that mother and father have for one another is the very love that he has for the two, individually. This leaves the parents' marital relationship colored by the idiosyncrasies of his self-perception. It is understandable, then, that witnessing the parents in intimation engenders powerful feelings and thoughts about himself. The child creates a dyad of mother and father to serve his own purposes, to provide desired ministrations, and to be the meaning of who he is as a person. Yet, increasingly, the child in his or her oedipal stage of development, between the ages of three and five or six years, comes to see that the mother and father are in a relationship not only of love and desire, but one that excludes their child. This is indeed a social dilemma, but between the ages of three and four its severity is yet to be encountered.

The relationship the child has had with each parent, separately, has provided the framework from which to expand his selfhood and solidify his boundaries as a differentiated person, Complexity ensues, however, when the child, now individuated, finds himself at the throes of a developmental crisis, acknowledging that his social world does not revolve around him as its hub. Significant persons have relationships to one another that may only indirectly or secondarily involve or effect him. In the all-important case of mother and father, their marital relationship is the center of the family circle and the child is faced with the vaguely perceived reality that mother and father have warm and tender feelings for one another in a relationship that in fact does not involve him. The marital bond stands on its own merit with its own purpose, function, and process. Hence, the triadic relationship is born and the oedipal situation is at the forefront.[3]

An inevitable rise in tension marks the oedipal phase of psychological and social development. The oedipal child's task is to accommodate the expanded world as he encounters it. Yet, maturationally, he is still dictated by a sense of illusory control over his world of things and people, a world that he perceives to have constructed himself. Therefore, he is yet to painfully learn that he must adapt to his exciting and demanding environment rather than the environment accommodate him. This fact of life raises tension, elicits anxiety, and poses an inherent conflict that during the oedipal phase of psychosocial development he will come to resolve. Resolution is no easy task; it is one that involves the aid of increasingly sophisticated self-defensive and protective mechanisms, as well as strengthened interpersonal skills.

The child to this point in his life has enjoyed the more simple and easily adaptive nature of two-person relationships. At the threshold of the oedipal phase of his psychological development the eager yet vulnerable child of three years is forced to relate to both parents not only individually, but as a triadic unit. This challenge is, to a small degree, welcomed by the child, although to a greater degree it is painful and trying.

The child continues to idealize his parents and is tantalized by the notion of entering the collective mother and father unit. Feeling increasingly vulnerable to the hardships and occasional onslaughts of the real world, the omnipotence that the young child had self-generated is defensively transferred to the newly created parental unit. Therewith, the child shares in the omnipotence he attributes to them, and draws from their combined strength and wisdom. Empathically attuned to their child, the parents foster a triadic constellation that encourages the child to experiment in his role.

Early in the oedipal phase of three to five or six years, the child's loving feelings for his parents do not pose a conflict, nor is the love for one parent seen to be in competition with that for the other. This will soon change. Joyfully, the child experiments by manipulating and managing mother and father as well as himself in juxtaposition to them within the triad. To a significant extent, the parents permit their socially practicing child to create a variety of patterns of family interaction. This is typically done in the context of the family's social play, and done for its pleasure not withstanding the valuable social learning experience it engenders for the child. With his expanding mental, perceptual, and social skills, the child wishes to direct himself and his parents in the fullest variety of relationship patterns. The result is a relational interchange much akin to the variegated, ever-shifting display of a colorful kaleidoscope. The child separates the mother and father, then puts them back together. He moves strategically inside the mother-father dyad, then pointedly moves out. Securing himself next to one parent and excluding the other, he then draws the excluded parent in to the included parent-child unit, and then proceeds to discard the previously included parent. The variety of displacements, reversals, and transformations choreographed by the child occur under the umbrella of empathically attuned parents who not only shore their parental relationship, but also delight in their loved one's expanding social activities. The child's social acumen enhances as do his mental and motor skills, and his reality sense refines.

It is not just the child's ego that advances to a new level of organization during the oedipal years. His ability to effectively utilize his body as an instrument of social relations increases. His strengthened motor skills permit the child to engage the world with greater physical agility and endurance, raising the child's awareness of his or her own body. Children of both sexes in their fourth year show interest in every nuance of their physical beings. He or she becomes aware of his or her personal existence. The child also begins to recognize his or her bodily attributes to be similar to either his or her father or mother. Comparing and contrasting the physical characteristics of the parents colors his or her perceptions and very often sensitively so. Among these characteristics are, for example, the color of one's hair and eyes, the possession of two hands and feet, the type of clothing worn, etc. Of great significance, too, the child notes that he or she either does or does not possess a penis. The child at this early age does acknowledge his or her gender, and is acutely aware of the similarities to and differences with both parents. The child's sexual identity is ushered in and is a result of increasing body awareness and functioning. Thus is set into motion, as created and generated by the child himself or herself, the Oedipus situation and its inherently related, personal dilemma.

As noted, from the child's perspective, he himself is the very engineer of this wonderful, though more complicated, social realm of mother, father, and child. Believing the triadic configuration to be of his own design, he views his creation as an extension of himself, and perceives the parental dyad in terms of that which he projects into them. The gratified and gratifying, as well as the loved and loving, child offers himself to his parents. He then reincorporates this experience into his own solidifying sense of a worthily loving and lovable person. Alternating between physical and emotional inclusiveness and exclusiveness in the parent's marital relationship, the child may feel powerless in his wish for complete control of the triad. The child longs for the return of the harmony felt earlier, but now experiences pain, sadness, anxiety, and fear. These feelings stem from an envy he has toward one parent in his desire for possession of the other. The child feels deprived and rejected when excluded from the parents' marital relationship. The oedipal aged child then struggles within his pliable mind with integrating the unpleasant feelings he has about the triangular family with the positive, loving feelings about the threesome. This struggle is the basis of the oedipal conflict.

At the age of three to four years, the child identifies with the parent of the same gender as a primitively wishful means of replacing this parent and forming an exclusive union with the parent of the opposite sex. The child attributes good and exciting characteristics to the dyadic relationship with the opposite-sexed parent and a less stimulating and impassioned view of the same-sexed parent is formed. Increasingly, the parent of the other gender becomes the object of his or her libidinal desire and to whom the child wishes to be forever attached. As identification with the parent of the same gender solidifies, the child desires to be more like this parent, not just to replace him or her, but to acquire the ability to capture the love of the parent of the opposite sex. In time, however, a rivalry is formed with the same-sexed parent, realistic and justified in the child's mind who wishes to discard one parent for the other. The triadic relationship of mother, father, and child becomes sexualized and rivalrous in nature.[4] This is a part of normal maturation, engineered by the child's developing personal, body, and social awareness, as well as the cognizance of a sexual identity. The child of the oedipal age is acutely attuned to the triangular significance of his or her perceptions, feelings, and activities.

An integral component of the child's identity structure is an exciting, though equally painful, recognition that he or she desires the parent of the other gender. One's person incorporates the acknowledgment of one's central wish—to have a longing desire for the love of the opposite-sexed parent while maintaining love for the same-sexed parent. Painful recognition comes when the child realizes that the parent of his or her desire has a desire of his or her own for the other parent. This holds true for both females and males. Envy results as the child agonizes over his or her aspiration for the parent who belongs to someone else. Despite the child's suffering, there is a positive side to this experience: The child's identity is inherently strengthened. The child's intense envy of the parent of the same gender creates a rivalry identification with this parent.

The boy's much desired mother turns from him in favor of intimation with father, the man to whom mother is romantically committed. This is a serious blow to the young child's self-esteem and he is spurred to compete with his father in the ultimate wish to capture mother's requiting love. Interestingly, the boy challenges father by identifying with him. In the child's fantasy, identifying with the rival allows for closer scrutiny of him and easier manageability of the triangular relationship. In the end, the boy's fantasy is that he will topple his rivalrous father and claim his mother's love.

In like fashion, the girl witnesses the object of her primary attachment, her mother, successfully claim father's love, the very person the girl wishes to claim for her own. The father's undeniable attention to mother and the mother's capacity to command his intimation result in the girl's narcissistic injury. The intensity of the blow induces the girl to actively compete with her original attachment figure for father's undivided love. As with the boy and his father, the girl's strategy is to identify with mother's prowess in hopes of securing for herself mother's talent for capturing father's unbridled attention. The girl strategically moves herself closer to her mother attempting to understand her and discern mother's magical ways.

A child finding himself or herself embedded in a triangular relationship with feelings of desire, envy, and frustration at the hands of an intense wish for someone who is unavailable creates the conflict of the Oedipus situation. The anxiety and anguish is similar for girls and boys, yet the experience is less intense for boys. The oedipal courses for both genders are qualitatively different by nature's design. The boy's primary attachment to his mother, as comforting as it has been, becomes a source of anxiety, viewing their relationship as a symbol of dependence, insufficiency, and stagnation. The boy is maturationally guided to turn from his mother and emulate his father to capture the attentions of a woman like his mother. In the oedipal phase, the boy's fantasy is that the woman will be none other than his mother. The primacy of the original attachment is and shall forever be upheld. Yet, it is the primary identification that the boy has with his mother and her strength, courage, and wisdom that prepares him to disengage her. The boy does not wish to sever the attachment to his loving and beloved mother. Rather it is his ambition to progress independently to become the man, like his father, who will win the heart of his mother.[5] Liberating himself from the mother inspires the boy to someday recapture her symbolically in adulthood.

The girl's venture is fraught with even more ambivalence. She, too, must disengage the mother-child matrix, but proceeds at a slower and more cautious pace. Just as the boy utilizing the loving primacy of the mother-child attachment as a springboard for his emancipation, the girl capitalizes on the identity constructed in relationship to her mother, developing a qualitatively different and perhaps stronger identification. After all, the mother and daughter are of the same gender, and gender identity is what crystallizes during the oedipal years.

The passivity of the girl's pre-oedipal experience, though more pronounced than with the boy, affords the girl the opportunity to identify with her mother in two ways. She identifies with both mother's self-denying protectiveness of her family and the mother's active independent strength. The dual identification with the maternal figure helps solidify both her sexual identity and the ability to activate it for the father who appropriately invites her intimation. The girl's identification with the more passive, self-sacrificing side of the mother who unfailingly serves, provides for, and protects her family, comprises the foundation on which she carefully constructs her self-vision to attract a man like her father.

Yet, the other side of the dual identification with the maternal figure mandates that the female child pursue eventual adulthood, womanhood, and the love of a man by mature adult means. This is the independent side of her mother of which the girl is becoming increasingly aware and the mother unquestionably has as her own place in the real, external world. Her daughter admires this fact and wishes to emulate her mother's activity toward accomplishment and acquisition. Indeed, one of these accomplishments and acquisitions is the procurement of the girl's own beloved father. It is from the primacy of love for mother that the girl pointedly directs her love to the father.

Seeking the love of her father is an ambivalent proposition for the oedipal girl, but by no means difficult to process. The female child of infancy and toddlerhood has an innate proclivity to heterosexuality and it is the father who is sought out in the triad. She believes it is her father who will satisfy her maturationally appropriate needs and wishes to step outside the mother-child dyad in search of social involvement with the other gender. Father has been the mysterious yet alluring person on the periphery and now it is time for her to seek him out, engage him, and experiment with him.

What the girl brings to her expanding relationship with her father is the goodness she feels within. The ego enhancing feelings she has about herself are acquired from her identification with her loving mother, and she delivers it to her father as a gift. It is here that the daughter and father secure their attachment. Although she desires the kind of love observed between her parents, the girl does not supplant mother for the exclusive love of the father. In fact, it is her love for both that engages her. While she increasingly directs her intimate attention to her father, the girl cautiously looks back to her mother seeking signs of success in reaching her goal.[6] She wishes not to topple her mother and claim her father, but establish her own identity as a person not at one with the mother, but as a similar yet separate person. Observing her mother as the girl relates to the father, the oedipal girl asks herself some developmentally important questions: Is mother concerned about my activity? If so, is mother envious of, or intimidated by, me? And moreover, am I in fact a person separate from my mother? If so, the girl perceives herself as a success, not only in winning the attention of father, but in establishing a clear demarcation between her and her mother. The distinction is not an expression of emotional and behavioral repudiation, but an affirmation of love for the mother.[7] This is an early expression of a feminine ideal.

The feminine ideal becomes an integral part of the girl's ideal self and therefore becomes a structural part of her ego.[8] By observing and identifying with her mother, she discovers what femininity means within her particular family circle. The mother facilitates the healthy feminine identification in her daughter. Comfortable with her own femininity and its personal and social expression, the facilitating mother naturally instills a similar comfort and security in her child. The girl is free to fantasize the capture of father's love and intimacy. She feels confident in her ability to do so with a realistic perception and sense of her own body and how her body can be used to engage the physical and social world.

It is hoped that the mother is sensitive to the nuances of her daughter's newly acquired social capacity and personal desire. Within the realm of a healthy marriage and family, mother knows she will not be supplanted by her daughter for her husband and need not be intimidated by her daughter's coquettish behavior. The mother should not feel injured when it seems as if she is being discarded as the girl infuses her father with love and selects him to be the target of her reciprocating intimations. The girl's age appropriate bid for liberation from mother and her attraction to her father is fraught with ambivalence. Anxiety is aroused as the girl acknowledges, however rudimentary in conceptualization, that she is envious of her own ideal—the mother. Yet, she has created for herself a rivalrous situation, becoming aggressive in her fantasy of replacing mother, and feeling guilty about destroying the very loving and loved person with whom she otherwise so endearingly identifies. The mother offers empathic reassurance and guidance in her appropriateness of social attraction to the parent of the other gender, and the girl comes to believe, in all her delight, that she does have father "wrapped around her little finger."

The image of the father is potent to his daughter for a number of reasons. As noted, there is an innate investment of even the very young female child in her father. Heterosexuality establishes itself early in the girl's life and psychosocial experience. The father is the selected person simply by virtue of his position in the family. Yet, the father is so much more than a merely accessible person. From the perspective of the four-year-old girl, he possesses two very much admired attributes: Separateness and freedom. Though he may have tender and loving relationships with his wife and daughter, the father nonetheless moves in and out of his relationships, seemingly at his own discretion and motivation. The girl sees herself as father's beloved daughter when and as he chooses. She wishes to arrange her social world to induce her father to choose her.

Freedom, too, is the ultimate goal of the girl's social arrangement. She does not wish for her father simply for acquisition's sake. The father is desired because he represents freedom in two ways. First, he is a free man who comes and goes indiscriminately and with the authority to define his own intimate relations with both his wife and daughter. Freedom is unquestionably appealing. Secondly, freedom, by definition to the oedipal aged girl, necessarily entails and is experienced by disengagement from the mother-child dyad.

Father's amenability to love and intimation with his daughter is founded specifically on two issues. First, the child is the very fruit of his creation and represents an integral and precious part of himself. Secondly, the nature of the father-daughter relationship, from its inception, is obviously different than that of the mother-daughter relationship. Because of father's auxiliary care giving service to the child, the life sustaining function simply does not exist for him as it does for the mother. The young girl has yet to form a strong identification with this person she so admires. The father has not yet been solidly internalized or represented in her mental world, and is therefore not subject to the vicissitudes of ambivalence, repression, and the duality of the gratifying and ungratifying aspects of the father. These are otherwise normal defensive maneuvers employed by the young ego. While the father is not the person from whose body the child is born, he is, nonetheless, the chosen one to facilitate and enrich the definition of who his daughter is to become.

By acknowledging his little girl's advances toward him as the object of desire, the father must graciously assume responsibility to gauge his activity in response to hers. Well within a socially appropriate context that fosters the girl's recognition, definition, and acceptance of her femininity, the father is delighted with the feminine coquetry of his daughter and provides her the much needed support as she struggles to maintain loyalty to her mother. She simultaneously grows in desire for the father. Sensitive to her envy of the mother, the father helps his daughter attenuate her rivalrous feelings. By being appropriately responsive to his little girl's enchantment and flirtation, he reveals that the mother is envious of her, too. Mother's envy strengthens the girl's identification with her and eases the burden experienced concerning displacing the mother and the hostility from the rivalry.

The young girl's overall definition of herself is blueprinted by the father who offers the optimal amount of emotional involvement and continued abeyance of his own regressive fantasies. The ideal father neither over nor under stimulates his child during this critical period of time. He serves as a model by displaying the appropriateness of close emotional and physical interplay, promoting the healthy identification an oedipal girl begins to form with her father. She learns to temper her intimate desires and proclivities without feeling either under challenged or overwhelmed. Through the course of the Oedipus period, it is the responsibility of both parents to facilitate their child's eventual renunciation of her bid for her father. By means of identification with the realities of her relationships with both parents, she must modify her wishes and humbly accept that she needs and wants the love of both parents individually and collectively, and that she must accept her father as the single sexual possession and possessor of her mother.

A man may not always be aware of what it is that makes him a man, nonetheless, he feels it every time he gazes into his daughter's eyes and holds her to his heart. His loving and beloved daughter is a reflection of his wife and his relationship with her. The father-daughter relationship is solid, yet the intimacy inherent in this attachment cannot be equaled to that of the male child and his mother. The relationship between the boy and his mother has as its foundation the original tie that psychologically expands in expression and meaning. The mother and son are intricately attached, and will forever be.

The male child in his oedipal years establishes a sense of masculinity based on how he asserts his developing cognitive faculties, social skills, psychomotor acquisitions, and bodily strength. The boy perceives himself firmly as a male. His perception is directly in reflection of how his mother defines maleness and masculinity within the context of her own life experiences. The mother has certain views and attitudes about men and manhood acquired from previous encounters. Her interpretation of these experiences influences her ability and willingness to acknowledge and accept masculinity in males. Mother takes pleasure in her young son's engagement.

The mother, too, attenuates her ambivalence by encouraging her son's masculine identifications on two fronts. First, by acknowledging and enjoying her husband's masculinity she provides a marital context in which her young son creates by observation, identification, and emulation, a perception of what it means to be male, express masculinity, and receive a woman's femininity. The mother who encourages her husband's masculinity strengthens the husband's male assertions. His maleness becomes an integral part of the boy's identification. Secondly, the mother is willing to engage her son in emotional and physical interplay that emphasizes the male component of his formulating identity. In appropriate contexts, a mother and son can relate to one another in ways that stimulate the boy to express his masculinity. The mother's mild seduction of her son not only helps delineate his inherent maleness, but also allows her to come to terms with her ambivalence, and perhaps naiveté, about her son's masculinity, as well as her perception of maleness in general. This is a tremendous learning experience for the mother who will acknowledge her progeny as one who will someday become a man. For him, she provides a fertile context in which he views himself as a male of his own identity.

It is the very masculinity with which the boy identifies in his father and generates within himself that ushers in the aspiring child's oedipal conflict. The loving mother is the object of his libidinous desires. The mother becomes sexualized and the father is now perceived as an obstacle to overcome. Identification with father, now illuminated by the maleness they share, is colored, from the boy's perspective, with competitiveness. The oedipal boy wants mother's exclusive attention.

Acknowledging the power of father's dominance, coupled with his witnessing of the mother's allegiance to her husband and the couple's mutual governorship of the family unit, leaves the boy feeling helpless and conflicted. In the child's nascence, he is still dependent on the two profoundly important persons in his life. The boy resolves the inherent conflict of the Oedipus triangle and comes to terms with the reality of his helplessness by forming an identification with both parents, internalizing the empathic, loving provisions they provide individually and collectively.

In spite of the father's dominance, he is still to some degree intimidated by the maturation of his son and the means by which he impresses his mother. The father recognizes that his wife's self-esteem is enhanced by their child, and their son is the creative manifestation of the mother's love for humankind and the person she once carried so carefully and securely within her womb. Now the boy advances in early step toward manhood. The promise of eventual manhood completes, for the hopeful mother, the cycle in the advancement of humanity and immortality. No doubt, the father can only step back and observe the profound significance of the primary relationship between the mother and son, and accept with awe and humility its supremacy.

The father, imbued by the pliable mind of the fledgling son with hostile intentions toward the boy, has only generous aims toward the son he so endears. The perceived rivalry is merely a reflection of the boy's own aggressive wishes toward his father. He finds them intolerable and therefore projects them into his father. This creates a mindful hardship for the child who not only needs to identify with both parents, but also loves them both dearly. He desires not to either discard or be discarded by his idealized father.

Experiencing and expressing affection for either parent creates loyalty conflicts within the young boy, fearing that love for either may connote repudiation of the other. The kind of relationship and interaction he chooses with his father assumes a different, though equally meaningful, quality than with his mother. He seeks his father as a friend, mentor, and protector. The boy discovers through his father how he can become a man someday. Normal intellectual and social development allows this event to unfold under the care of a loving father.

A newfound desire for companionship with the "good" father rather than with the "bad" father of rivalrous conflict compels the boy to experience humility. The humility is attenuated and made more tolerable by the empathic father who does not misuse his authority to subjugate his son. He, conversely, revels in the ideal to which his son attributes him. Glowing with pride, the father adopts a degree of his own humility. After all, even though his wife adores and admires their son in a uniquely different way than she does her husband, their son is also, in part, of the father's creation. Yet, the father knows that the mother-son relationship remains largely outside of his domain. The empathically attuned father understands and accepts his son's personal struggle in finding his position in the family triangle. The father comes to be seen by his son as the ally and protector that he has indeed always been. The boy of age five or six, at the end of the oedipal phase, is in resolution of this conflict and views his father in perfective form. He idealizes his father in all his strength, wisdom, excitement, and loveliness. No longer rivaling the father, the boy appreciates the ideal of his father and forms a strong identification with that ideal. Resultingly, the boy acquires a more keen sense of his male identity and the role which that gender identity necessitates in interpersonal relations. He begins to understand and appreciate not only his new image and role with his mother and father, but with all other persons as well. Ultimately, upon reaching his own manhood, he will understand what it means to be a good man in loving relation to a good woman.

In addition to the more matured identification with the ideal father, the boy transforms his identification with his beloved mother. He identifies with the mother, relinquishing his dependence on her and ceases the libidinalization of his mother sexually. A masculine identification with the father permits the boy to strengthen and profess his masculinity in relation to mother as the woman he continues to admire and love, but in deference to his father. He anticipates a future with the love of a woman much like his mother. This organizes a new and more sophisticated identification with the mother, and affords the boy new relationship potentials with his father.

By the time the child has reached his or her sixth birthday, the triangle is no longer shaded with or driven by envy, rivalry, and conflict. The child acquires the intellectual capacity to perceive, assess, and engage the world and its reality. His or her place in the family assumes a different role, function, and purpose. To the benefit of both the family circle and the individuated child, he or she becomes more competent, and therefore more effective, in social acclaim.

With an increased sense of competency develops a rise in self-regard. Transferring what is good in the family circle into his or her self-structure, the child maintains an internal sense of well-being, reminiscent of the feeling of being at one with the mother.

The endearing identifications that both the young girl and boy develop in relation to their parents enliven the mother and father, reinforcing their parental love and approval. Unquestionably, all parents are gratified by their child's emulation of them. The child, though not consciously aware of his or her imitations of the idealized parents, is testimony to the potency of the intersubjective, relational quality and nature of the identification process. What mother does not take great delight when her son tells her that she is the most beautiful and wonderful woman in the whole wide world? What father does not sink to submissive modesty in that his precious little girl has more influence over him than does anyone else? Transversely, the good father, too, relishes the "chip off the old block" that he perceives his son to be, as does the good mother whose daughter proclaims her intention to be the good wife and mother that her mother is.

Chapter Seven

Love and the Adolescent Experience

By the age of six years, both the male and female child have typically traversed the oedipal path and resolved its inherent conflict. The child no longer perceives himself to be the core of the family triad, though earlier in the oedipal years, he believed it necessary, in fact his function, to manage and manipulate the relationship patterns among them. No longer is the ultimate aim to secure and maintain the intimation of the parent of the opposite gender, but to integrate into the developing awareness of his own sexuality, his mother's sexuality and femininity, and his father's sexuality and masculinity. Determining one's position in the midst of this more complex arrangement is a matter of creativity and personal engineering. Just as the oedipal child believes that he has created the other-than-mother-and-me configuration of the family triangle, he now, at the Oedipus resolution, creates with his own internal and relationship resources, his very own identity.[1] Though still tied to the loving significance of the mother and father, he is now a distinctive self in loving continuance of mother and father. A person in his own right, the child has a unique identity, inclusive of a sexual identity with his own desires, wishes, fantasies, anxieties, fears, and an overall perception of the wondrous world in which he lives and of which he is an integral part. The child's social world is no longer one to be managed and manipulated, rather one to be accommodated and with which to be negotiated.

Love and intimacy persist in the family of the six-year-old child, however they are now energized by the child's own identity. The parents increasingly serve in support of their child's ego, but the nature of the child's emotional attachment changes because of the child's notably decreasing dependence on his parents for his view of himself and of other persons, as well as his diminishing interest in his mother and father. The parents do not cease to be important or intriguing, but the child now discovers new interests in siblings, classmates, teachers, neighbors, and others, creating the genesis of his place as a person among persons.

The source of the child's personal concept and esteem transfers from the loving and empathic parents who effectively mirror their child's self-image to the child himself. Having internalized and identified with the parents' loving and caring qualities and established them as part of his personality, he is now more able to direct, govern, discipline, and protect himself. The child becomes his own monitor, judge, and jury, as well as his own commender, appraiser, and affirmer. Less as a mirror in which the child finds his ideal self, the parents are more of an outside agency to be enlisted for advice and aid. The parents' perfection, wisdom, and values are still idealized, but more as a part of the self, becoming a significant source of pride and energy for the child as he struggles to interface with the social and physical world of greater magnitude than he can yet fathom.

At this stage of the child's development, the parents intuitively and timely reduce the physical intimacy they express toward their child. Their feelings are not diminished, rather, they must accept their child's maturation and the age appropriate need to secure their affection by means of his developing verbal skill. The child of six years is sufficiently adept to express and receive love by both language and physical contact. Additionally, as his sexual awareness of the self and others solidifies, he also learns from his parents that he, too, must respect others' privacy and ownership of their bodies.

In this light, parents readily accept their child's changing view of them. The child is both able and willing to see his parents as persons with desires, goals, perceptions, and thoughts unique to them and different from his own. He realizes that his mother and father have their own directions in life, means of interfacing their environments, and their own inadequacies and shortcomings. With this increasing maturational awareness, their child relinquishes his physical desire for the parents and exhibits more personal competence and confidence.[2] His self-esteem rises, and he feels even more worthy of his parents' love and admiration. Reciprocally, his parents' self-worth heightens as they witness their child's developmental success.

During the oedipal years, parents begin to see their child developing a unique personality, and by the age of six he is a person of his own being. The child's pride in himself begets parental pride in his accomplishments. The parents intuitively support their loved one as he experiences inevitable disruptions in his personal integrity as he interfaces life's normal hardships. The child's sense of cohesiveness is contingent on the preservation of mother's and father's availability and guidance through difficult times. The child fears losing his parents; moreover, he fears losing their love. However, parents are empathically attuned, if only unconsciously, to their loved one's anxiety and they assure their accessibility to their still vulnerable child.

As a precaution against losing parental love, the child taps into his own internal reserve of self-esteem and personal worth in two ways: The child's expanding ego gives him the tools to build competence in his interface with the external world, and, secondly, through the internalization of his parents' shared wisdom, values, and strength, and his solid identification with these personal qualities, the child idealizes himself in all of his proficiencies. He therewith comes to recognize himself as a person worthy of love from others as well as from within. As the child lives up to his ideal self, he increases his self-esteem and self-respect. The ideal self, or ego-ideal, from the internalization of his parents' ideals, provides the basis for channeling the child's energies to activities of the world beyond his family, relieving the parents of his infantile attachment.

The child of six years finds his or her social life much easier to negotiate. A relative ease of relating to mother and father individually and collectively is fostered by the child's ever-strengthening and solidifying sense of personhood—a person unique to oneself and among other persons in his and their distinction. The child identifies himself as a person whose ability and propensity to love and be loved is contingent on his ability and opportunity to love himself. Self-love is a personal accomplishment of great magnitude lending the child personal esteem and purpose. The child perceives himself as a person of value delightfully equal to that of his parents.

Between the ages of five or six years and the onset of puberty, the child draws on his or her newly acquired and expanding personal assets. Social interaction is relatively easy, due in part to the desexualization with which the child engages others in social interplay.[3] The child has acquired a firm sense of who he or she is, what his or her gender is, and what role that identity plays in the family circle. The realization that mother and father are not to be pursued or held in sexual or possessive desire provides great relief to the child who can now engage the social and physical world with a sense of freedom. Much of the love that the child now receives comes in the form of praise for his personal and social accomplishments. This felt praise and love is both summoned from within as self-acclaim and derived from without as parental and community commendation. The more praise, both internal and external, the child experiences, the more he feels worthy of love, and can offer it in return to the important people in his life.

The relatively conflict-free world of childhood typically comes to an abrupt halt with the onset of puberty. Pubescence marks a critical transition from the simplicity of childhood with relatively less instinctual drive and social demands to the forthcoming flood of hormonal release with its social ramifications. From a purely personal perspective, the adolescent is at a pivotal point in his wish and need for the maintenance of infantile ties to the loving and ministering parents and the simultaneous biological, psychological, and social push toward the maturity of adulthood which he so ardently wishes to secure. In the teen's view, adulthood exemplifies and holds promise for, in its purest and most ultimate form, the very embodiment of freedom, independence, autonomy, and the self-affirmation that is resultingly claimed. The child at early adolescence does have some semblance of recognition of the harsh realities of the adult world. He witnesses the actualities of adulthood as they are experienced by his parents and his friends' parents. A child's sense of omnipotence must be relinquished, lest it be destroyed by life's complexities, to claim a viable position in the adult arena. The adult experiences a void within for failed achievements and unmatched ideals, and the adolescent child recognizes the emptiness in the lives of his mother and father. He foresees, partially in reality and partially in fantasy, the abundance of life that awaits in the proclamation of adulthood, while hauntingly foreseeing the inevitable vicissitudes of personal insubstantiation that is part of the adult experience.[4]

Ultimately, reality overshadows ambivalence confirming that childhood has passed. The adolescent must relinquish his original ties with the mother and father as he sets foot onto the threshold of adulthood in like form of his parents. This maturity is unavoidably fraught with sadness and pain, mourning the loss of a precious and integral part of oneself—the primacy of the mother-infant attachment.[5] The adolescent boy or girl must relinquish the libidinous attachment to the original loved one, the unconditionally ministering mother. The process of separation - individuation occurs in the toddler years and is experienced again in the teen years. This second break from the parents is necessary. Liberation and independence, be it at toddlerhood or adolescence, comes at a sufferable price.

Nonetheless, there is for the teenager a biological, psychological, and social push toward facing the world of intimate relations with a maturing mind, spirit, and body. Indeed, the adolescent's personality is strengthening for coping with instinctual drives, social demands, and personal insecurities. Yet, paradoxically, the ego is weaker in its vulnerability for having relinquished infantile ties in aspiring favor of an adult personality. This new state of being is acutely susceptible to the onslaughts created by hormonal changes and desires for intimacy based on his or her newly acquired sexual abilities and proclivities. Turning away from childhood security, the teenager yearns for support from whomever is available and amenable. The vulnerability of the teen stems from, for the most part, that he has but himself as a source of support. Inasmuch as he has internalized the caring and loving functions of his parents, he will by their distant guidance experience a vicarious yet certain support from within.

The realities of adulthood, as experienced to some degree in early adolescence, require the youngster to modify the image of his parents as being all-powerful and all-knowing. Yet, the adolescent continues to perceive his parents in a positive light inspite of their shortcomings. Unquestionably, adolescence is fraught with trial and tumultuous disruption of the entire family's cohesion. The maturing adolescent repudiates his parents' mores, values, and ideals in favor of his own.[6] Ironically, his own ideals are decidedly based on the identifications he has formed with his mother and father. Indeed, the adolescent disclaims his parents, frequently in the defiance of the mother and father. However, the teen neither defeats nor destroys them. The reciprocation of the family's love and acceptance endures.

The degree to which the adolescent disavows parental ideals depends on the degree to which he is able to formulate an idealizing parental image within his mind and transform his own self-image in light of this internalization. The teenager, expectedly, disavows certain aspects of the parental images. He realistically perceives imperfections in his parents, and having identified with them, realizes his own paralleled imperfections different than, though equal to, those of his parents. The teen's identifications with the parents become more sophisticated, mature, and selective as he abandons the standards and mores of his childhood ego-ideal. In replacement, he begins to construct a new ego-ideal, founded on both an internal self-guidance and the identifications with the parents that are deemed useful.[7] Typically, the new ego-ideal is based on love, intimacy, and attachment.

Parents are now decreasingly viewed by their teenaged child as the source of personal stability and identity. Although the teenager continues to view them in idealized form, the idealization is more reality based and more intellectually determined. The parents' personality characteristics deemed valuable by their aspiring child are greatly appreciated, and, in fact, are called upon to support him as he delineates his identity in comparison with and contrast to them.

In all of his yet weakness, as the teenager tenuously makes the transition from childhood to adulthood, he finds stabilization and support from within. For most teens, self-esteem is precariously maintained, yet the regulation of personal value is increasingly generated by one's own internal organization. Much of what was once idealized in the parents now comes to be idealized in oneself. Love for the parents transforms to love for oneself, not in supplantation, but in precious identification. Love for oneself is the sine qua non, the very essence and expression, of love for the mother and father. Only in the capacity of loving one's parents does one come to love oneself. This does not

change during the tumultuous period of adolescence. Indeed, adolescent repudiation of parents and their ideals is not born from disdain, as it oftentimes
appears. Rather, it is the ultimate expression of the painful "letting go" of the
mother's and father's influence in favor of the enlightening gain of a distinct,
respectable, and honorable self-identity. Parental love is the very cornerstone
of the emancipation process and the elemental base on which a child's liberation succeeds.

When the adolescent does not succeed in drawing support, esteem, and
affirmation from within, he will direct his attention to those outside of his
family to idealize, acquire personal value, and confirm his identity. However, in the normative process, the teenaged boy or girl draws inwardly,
narcissistically aimed and preoccupied.[8] As a result, the pursuit of goals is
self-fulfilling. This inward involvement is appropriate to the teen embarking
upon adulthood, knowing that maturation is now in his own hands and of his
own accord. Inherent in his endeavor is the importance of maintaining the image of himself as not only a viable being, but as one who is both loving and
loved, not only by the parents but by significant others. This reinforces the
adolescent's narcissistic appeasement as a means of countering the demean-
ing onslaught to the integrity of his still formulating identity.

Maintaining a personal balance is contingent on the preservation of the
teenager's ego-ideal. The closer his personal ideal is in relation to reality, the
more likely the teen will succeed in striving for and attaining his personal
goals. The ideal self will command the acknowledgement, respect, and admiring love of his parents.

The adolescent soon finds that idealizing the self is insufficient in maintaining a healthy self-perception and equilibrium. Relationships with peers
help the teen establish and affirm his identity, providing for him a sense of
belonging, and maintaining a sense of well-being. The peer group the adolescent chooses to idealize becomes an integral part of his ego-ideal. Relinquishing parental ties and letting go of the attachment so lovingly cherished entails
a tremendous loss. The loss from relinquishing parental ties is not only one
of shared intimacy, but a loss of the teen's own sense of the self. Now the
adolescent mourns the loss of this intimation and ego support, and replaces
it with intimacy and support from both himself and the peer group.[9] The
strengthening and expanding of parental internalizations, along with a new
idealization of the values, mores, and goals of the group of contemporaries
help construct the healthy ego-ideal. In particular, teenagers locate and appreciate the peer group attributes that address and correct the very attributes
of the parents determined to be disappointing and insufficient. The adolescent
experiences these inadequacies not only in the actual relationship with his
parents, but also as part of himself. Paradoxically, the teenager also shares

a remarkable ability and tendency to gyroscopically locate in the newly idealized peers certain characteristics found in the parents. This search for familiarity occurs unconsciously to the adolescent, for most teens will not admit to striving for ideals supported by the parents. However, unconscious idealization serves as clear testimony to the tenacity and cohesiveness of the earlier formed attachment of the adolescent child to his parents.

With a newly structured ideal on which to base his strivings and promote his identity, the adolescent gratefully accepts support from his peer group as they guidedly or misguidedly influence his identity. He forms trial identifications with his peers, typically transient in nature, that serve either developmental progression or regression. Identifications with the mores of the peer group may be firm and highly emotionally charged, but tend to be of a superficial quality. These invested identifications encourage the teen to sublimate his biological and social drives by channeling aggression and sexual desires into socially acceptable venues such as sports, music, academia, hobbies, and social causes. Seldom are adolescent identifications comprised of sexual activities.

What the adolescent seeks from his contemporaries are group activities and goals that will support and enhance his perfect self—his ego-ideal. He devours admiration and acceptance from his peers. A degree of commonality and belongingness is what the teenager needs to maintain a sense of personal dignity and to balance a precariously perceived identity. Teens find comfort in shared experiences.

Involvement with the peer group includes a commitment to its all-important social membership. Concurrently, however, the teen has an equal commitment to his own conscience, value system, and the ideals consistent with their dictations. Self-criticism and personal responsibility are determined by his conscience as it has developed in his formative years.

As moral proscriptions falter, the adolescent is biased toward falsely idealized, romanticized, and wish fulfilling perceptions of himself and others. This event can lend itself to the acting-out of emotionally intense, yet personally superficial, sexual desires. Ideally, the adolescent learns to transact his relationships based on accurate images of himself and others, and attenuates narcissistically glamorized views of his relationships that may promote sexual inclination. The idealization of peers and idols serves to effectively transform the teen's idealized parental images into the more mature adult idealization of the self. The adolescent's new social world provides a substitute for the family unit offering a sense of belongingness and someone with whom to share a mutual loyalty. Mourning the loss of parental ties leaves the adolescent vulnerable to increased longing for attachment and belongingness. The ego is subject to impoverishment, and with the experience of periodic and perhaps intense emptiness, the teenager seeks at least temporary relief from his peers.

Still a child at heart and in spirit, the adolescent wishes to simply love and be loved. Venturing into the adult world is a precarious and frightening proposition. What he longs for is someone with whom, like his mother and father that he must now relinquish, he can identify in his own relationship of security and mutuality. Commonality with the peer group and a shared commitment to its chosen ideals engenders in the adolescent a sense of inclusiveness, bonding, and trust.

What appears to be an external emotional investment is, upon closer inspection, merely a reflection and representation of what is being experienced internally. Personal investment in others serves more narcissistic aims and goals and is the vehicle in which the adolescent fosters his self-interest. This is not selfishness by any definition, however. The emotionally craving teen may well commit himself wholly to the cause of his peer constituency. Additionally, his turning inward to strengthen his personal esteem is an age appropriate phenomenon that serves as a temporary refuge and refueling station from which the venturing teen springs into adulthood. Self-interest and interest in others are amalgamated into a perceived single entity for the adolescent in transition between childhood and adulthood, recapitulating the sense of attachment he encountered during infancy and toddlerhood. Boundaries between himself and others temporarily blur and the images of the self and others merge. The teen is not certain of what is he and not he, of what is good for him and good for others, or of who he really is and what it is that he wants. An uncertain identity is due in part to a depleted ego and a lack of firm differentiation between himself and others.[10] Both are typical experiences of the adolescent.

Puberty is a crisis for the teenager that heightens his self-experience. The pubertal teen is acutely aware of what is happening to his or her body, though the awareness is seldom accompanied by comprehension. There is a sharpened perception of, and intensified attention to, stimuli that emanate from within the body. These stimuli are relatively benign. Yet, the minor aches and pains or the more critical menstrual experience or easily erected penis becomes an immediate concern for the surprised pubertal child. Everything that transpires within the body, along with the teen's feelings about it, is perceived as a threat to his personal stability and confounds his already tenuous identity. The heavily taxed adolescent is in a hyper state of alertness to every internal and external nuance of his being and is resultingly anxious at almost all times.

Physical maturity, heightened self-awareness, and sexual pronunciation, all ushered in at puberty, create an entirely new self-context, a new self in transformation from the prepubertal child. The teenager integrates all past experiences of attachment to loved ones into his current experience of sexual maturity. This transcends physical maturation and incorporates a necessarily profound psychological change in his sense of self. The body is not just different; it has an entirely new meaning and emphasis. His body's definition is now linked intricately and intimately to how the adolescent views himself as a person, be it positive or negative, and how his body translates to a perception of his newly acquired sexuality, viewed similarly as something either positive or negative, normal or abnormal.[11] The body of childhood had been merely a receptacle of needs and desires. Now, at the throes of pubescence, the body becomes the highly active force of sexual fantasy and behavior.

With the onset of puberty, the adolescent's body and sense of self become intertwined in a manner that had not existed since the oedipal years. The young child discovers his or her gender identification, and now, the pubertal teen rises to a new intellectual acknowledgment of not only his or her genitalia, but also of their amazing functions. The organization of the self is, with the advent of puberty, a sexual organization. The teen's personhood inherently includes his or her physically developing genitalia.

The importance of a healthy and stable self-concept is again determined by his identification with his mother and father. As an equally loving person who desires to express his love to others in attachment, he has a gentle and protective perception of his and others' bodies, as well as a sense of self and others. Ideally, the adolescent will love, respect, and accept his body, just as his parents had. With a positive view of himself, he matches and promotes his perceptions to those persons with whom he chooses to be intimate. The early feelings of love and acceptance acquired from his mother and father are internalized and transformed into the same tender feelings the teen has for himself. The body, in all its self-expression and self-meaning, is the very container of the love he experiences in its conceptual entirety.

Acknowledgment and acceptance of sexual identity and maturity, significantly determined by the experiences of sexuality, are no easy tasks for the typical teen. The teenager is now able to give a both conscious and unconscious meaning to his or her existence as a person, particularly as a sexual person. This meaning is colored significantly by the parents and their view of their beloved child. Yet, inherent in the normal vicissitudes of adolescent development, the meaning of one's existence is determined in great part by his or her biology. Biochemical and hormonal changes that have nothing to do with the parent-child relationship dictate undeniable realities that acutely effect the adolescent's perception of himself or herself. Sexual primacy for the male teenager means that he has the ability to experience a penile erection, produce semen, and ejaculate the sperm ladened semen with penile stimulation. The result is his capacity to impregnate a female and conceive the next generation of human being. For the female teenager, the primacy of sexuality involves the ability to produce eggs, ovulate, have them become fertilized, and gestate in the overall process of procreation.[12] The biology of one's existence is indeed a maturational smack in the face to the adolescent whose childhood is quickly disappearing and who is required to psychologically integrate his or her sense of body into the total concept of himself or herself.

Periodic states of panic and anxiety set in and establish the typical psychological condition of the adolescent. The anxiety is rooted in the lack of understanding of what is happening to himself or herself physically. Most parents choose not to instruct their children about the normalcy and meaning of biophysiological maturity, nor is it taught sufficiently in school. Additionally, the anxiety also has as its source the inevitable ambivalence the teen feels about himself as a person and about his strengths and weaknesses. Teenagers of both genders may feel a heightened sense of potency and pride in their body's recent acquisitions and will often express their splendor. However, the teen also fears these very achievements and experiences guilt with every expression. The task for the ambivalent teenager is to temper both his perceived strengths and shortcomings and amalgamate them into a unified whole.

The skills a child acquires during the years prior to adolescence come into question with the advent of puberty. The vulnerable teenager becomes hypersensitive to his ambivalently perceived self and the inadequacies and susceptibilities which can frequently overshadow his aptitudes and accomplishments. Some teens, fearful or anxious about their bodily changes turn inward and withdraw from family and peers, becoming narcissistically invested. This protective function is a means of attempting to understand one's psychological and bodily self by focusing attention on it. Other teens defend against the anxiety by directing their attention to cognitive and psychomotor skills such as gymnastics, dance, music, hobbies, and academics. These sublimating activities lend the eager teen the opportunity to discharge both the aggressive and libidinal energies that surge during adolescence.

Aggressive tendencies are easier to attenuate for both male and female adolescents because of available means of discharge within and among their peer groups. Group activity in a variety of forms, including "hanging out," hold potential for both healthy and unhealthy sublimation. Feelings of love and intimacy, on the contrary, are uneasily experienced and expressed. This is due in great part to the role that sexual feelings and functions play. During childhood, one's awareness of his or her body focuses principally on protecting it and its sexual organs without investing much attention in them. With the advent of puberty, interest is now directed toward the sexual organs and the body as a whole in process and function. The teenager is not only aware of but sensitive to the nuances of his or her sexual organs—what they can do and the internal bodily experiences created.

Love, intimacy, and the longing for attachment during adolescence include sexual identification and desire. During post-oedipal childhood, feelings and expressions of love and intimacy, and the attachments therewith formed, are relatively free of sexual impulses. The teenager, however, must integrate and come to terms with love and eroticism. Warm, tender, loving feelings have sexual overtones, and there is a heightened awareness of sexual desire. The male adolescent is typically quicker to meet these terms partly because of both social and cultural allowances, if not expectations, that the young man takes pride in expressing his sexual prowess. This is facilitated by the biological fact of the teen boy's immediate exposure to his own genitals' readiness for erection. The sexual implications in group activities imbue the male and female teen with anxieties and feelings that are inherently troubling, including the resurgence of oedipal feelings and incestuous thoughts either consciously or unconsciously experienced.[13] The fear of regression to the state of passivity and dependence encountered normatively during toddlerhood is also a source of anxiety. The teen's goal is to progress toward differentiation and emancipation as an adult in his or her own right. Love, intimacy, and attachment involve, by normal vicissitude, partial and temporary regressions despite the teen's efforts to thwart them.

The integration of eroticism with genuine desire for intimacy with another typically takes longer for the female adolescent. Socio-cultural factors play a vital role in the girl's expected suppression of sexual expression. Additionally, the girl at menarche has significantly more and intense physiological and hormonal changes with which to reckon, taking a heavy toll on the teen girl faced with the sharp reality of womanhood. The girl's anatomical transformations and maturation command a certain more attention to her body and internal processes. She is taxed with the necessary acknowledgement of a maturing body along with the maintenance of a psychological equilibrium in face of this maturation.

The ability to establish and maintain psychological balance in the midst of nature's biological upheaval varies notably from person to person. Every teen girl has a unique personality with which to contain, organize, and express the mandated changes of menarche. Some female adolescents have a tumultuous experience while for others, the vicissitudes of menarche comprise a proud and joyful encounter with a heightened sense of personal esteem and pending adulthood. Understandably, most fall in between the two extremes, leaving the girl feeling a mixture of excitement, trepidation, elation, despair, strength, and weakness.

With the appropriate family support, the girl will be able and willing to seize the encouraging and dignifying opportunity of menarche to advance her new identity as a young woman with its pronunciation of femininity, and take pride in her feminine ways. Her self-assertion is facilitated by her body concept, not singularly, but by how her burgeoning body correlates with and embellishes her personality as the ultimate expression of her personhood. Accepting herself as having an equally strong sense of mind, body, and spirit, engenders for the girl an ultimate sense of femininity and sexual individuality. Therewith, she cherishes a true faith and trust in her ability to experience both sexual pleasure and fulfillment when the time comes.

Implicit in her new individuality, in loving identification with her mother and loving acceptance from her father, she is now a person in her own right. She modifies her self-ideal and includes expanding elements from female peers and admired older women such as teachers, neighbors, family friends, and extended family members. The girl notices that she is, for example, taller or shorter than her mother, has a different color or shade of hair and eyes, has breasts of a different shape and size, and a smile and gait all her own. She relishes both the likeness to and differences from her mother. This distinction offers the young woman the impetus to promulgate her own identity.

In even more personal and intimate terms, the teen girl takes with self-respect and dignity great delight in learning that something as detailed as her menstrual cycle is, in fact, succinctly personal and unique. The pattern of her cycle differs from all other females, including the length of time of her periods, the length of time between periods, the manner in which physical displeasure is experienced, and the manner in which she must care for her menstruating body. Similar to that of a young male, sexual awareness for the teen female extends from mere anatomical acknowledgement to that of both function and process. Indeed, the sexual organs and the means by which they function become an integral and highly prized component of the entire female identity.

The adolescent's wish is to love and be loved. In both passive and active measure, the teenage boy and girl long for ongoing contact with someone who holds promise for continuing, in more advanced form, the love and intimacy that was found in the secure attachment to the parents. This ultimate achievement is the means by which the teenager demarcates and adheres to his or her outer reality. A strong and stable reality sense of one's both internal experiences and external relationship encounters is essential to the adolescent's struggle to find and maintain himself or herself in pathway to adulthood. During the adolescent transition from childhood to adulthood, the teen maintains a fervent wish to be passively held, nurtured, and contained. Yet, the instinctual aim is to actively pronounce oneself in the context of one's bodily and sexual function. The teen's purpose is to fend off the loneliness and emptiness so commonly experienced during adolescence while attenuating the realistic fear of close, intimate, social relationship.

While the developmental processes of love and intimacy are served well by actual relationships with other persons, fantasy also aids in establishing contact with desired others, especially in the realm of sexual desire and expression. Fantasy comprises the bridge from one's inner self to actual persons in the external world. Still psychologically unequipped to engage in mature sexual activity, the adolescent safely invests in his or her own body as it is directed in fantasy to another person with whom he or she desires to be intimate. Fantasy aids identity formation by imagining oneself in intimate relations with another.[14]

The search for love through himself and beloved others is easily managed by the teen with the use of fantasy. Because it is a prerequisite to love and feel secure with oneself in order to love and feel comfortable with another in intimacy, sexual activity for the teenager, be it in fantasy or actuality, must be founded on a solid sense of self. And because the sense of self is precariously established during adolescence, the use of fantasy in sexual relations provides a safe mechanism for finding the desired other person and for finding oneself. In fantasy, the adolescent creates his own scenario, thereby permitting himself to return to reality at will. He invests erotic feelings in continuously self-determined, circular shifts between himself and the other person, internalizing the desired other and strengthening his ego. Fantasy helps the adolescent give up the beloved parents in favor of creating new love objects under the dictates of age appropriate maturation.

There is a natural tendency to fantasize about a relationship in trial and error before engaging in actual events. The teen will cautiously acknowledge his sexual capabilities and tendencies, even though there is a psychological and biological drive to activate them. The trial of being intimate with another person through imagination affords the eager, yet cautious, teen the chance to experiment mentally with the pleasure derived from self-stimulation of the genitals.

Fantasy and masturbation permit the adolescent to openly express the intimate desire for another while containing the desires within himself or herself. The mental mastery of erotic thoughts of sexual intercourse helps the adolescent organize his or her feelings and impulses, and to integrate them into what he or she wishes for in intimacy.

The natural outgrowth of masturbation with fantasy gives the adolescent opportunity to attentively observe himself. Self-observation takes many avenues; one of which is to formulate an image of one's bodily self. The teenager struggles with not only acquiring a stable body image, but one that is also liked and respected. Fantasy affords him not only the opportunity, but also the likelihood that he will come to idealize his bodily self just as his parents had facilitated his overall self-acceptance and admiration as a child. The idealized body image, however, does not match the actual body image until adulthood is attained. As the young adult experiences actual sexual relations, the ideal body and the real body images coalesce. Maturity and adulthood identity are only then achieved.

The younger child uses fantasy as an appropriate and healthy tool to link himself to the outside world of people, things, and events, and to learn trial and error activity and cause and effect relationships. For the adolescent, fantasy and masturbation facilitate sexual pleasure giving and receiving, feelings of intimacy, and eventual attachment and love to and with an actual other person. They also serve to bridge the use of identification with another as a way of relating intimately to the other, as was in childhood, with independent thought, desire, and activity. Self-observation, reinforced by sexual fantasizing and self-stimulation, aids the adolescent's ability to ward off anxiety, fear, and the psychological danger of sexuality. Self-observation creates a sense of personal intuition and perceptivity as to how to understand one's own internal sensations and impulses, and also to understand those same experiences in the partner and how he or she relates to his or her own sexuality. Sensitivity and empathy for oneself and the other are reinforced. Through masturbation and fantasy, as well as actual sexual relations, the adolescent establishes and validates for himself or herself a personally and socially appropriate and acceptable masculine or feminine identity. This achievement hinges greatly on the way the teenager perceives and contends with his or her own fantasies and the masturbation activity. In a healthy sense, the male and female teen uses masturbation and fantasy to attenuate aggressive tension and excessive erotic drive, therewith establishing an attitude toward a vision of a partner who is considerate, affectionate, sensitive, and personally esteemed.[15]

Fantasy with masturbation serves to determine which type of erotic thoughts, feelings, sensations, and impulses are tolerable to his or her sense of conscience and morality. The mature adolescent integrates these tempered experiences into his or her view of what a sexual person should be in match with his or her ideal self.

The adolescent boy, more so than the girl, typically uses fantasy with self-stimulation to safely separate his erotic urges from his genuinely tender and sentimental feelings. He fantasizes about women unknown to him as a way of assuaging guilt and to refrain from compromising the integrity of a female known to him. Pornography serves this purpose effectively. The teen boy, short of psychological maturity, tends to view women in terms of "good" and "bad," parallel in his perception to a female who is respectively either asexual or sexual. With maturity in late adolescence or early adulthood, he fuses the two sexual urgencies of eroticism and tenderness to form an appreciation and respect for his partner and her femininity.

The adolescent girl, too, typically directs her fantasies and masturbation activities toward males she doesn't know. Having actual access to a fantasied partner is not necessary, nor is it preferred. However, the female teen is more likely to introduce an element of romance and ecstatic love to her fantasies, feeling deep love for the nonactualized partner. The feeling of loving and being loved in an intimate and romantic way is what is pleasurable to the girl's amorous desires. The fantasies are, though significantly disguised to avoid incestuous guilt, reflective of certain elements of the fantasied and actual relationships she has with her father. It is a more tenuous task for the adolescent girl to let go of her emotionally tinged, paternal ties than it is for the male.

Self-stimulation during erotic fantasy does not focus on the genitalia in the same way for the female that it does for the male. Stimulation and imagery of her and her partner's genitals lean toward her fantasy of becoming both a woman in truly loving concert with a man and being ultimately capable of conception and reproduction with a lifelong lover. The female's internal and less observable genitals tend to be of great interest and mystery to the girl on the brink of womanhood. The capacity for motherhood, even if never actualized, and perhaps, feared, is at the helm of the teen girl's imaginative processes.

Being faced with the task of loosening ties to the parents in favor of securing emotional attachment to significant others is not only a difficult chore for adolescents, it is one that a person never fully accomplishes. In great part, the common depressed moods of adolescence are due to the mourning of the loss of primary love and the relationships inherent in the earliest years of life and carried so warmly and carefully through childhood. As it is difficult to mourn the loss of a loved one via separation or death, it, too, is with hardship to give up a part of oneself to which one has been so intricately and intimately tied and identified. Now, with the advent of biological maturity, this precious part of oneself must be given up.

As the older adolescent seeks a partner, he or she chooses someone who conforms to and is reminiscent of, however disguised, the nature of the relationships had with the mother and father. It is typical to endow one's new love object with the characteristics of one's earlier, indeed earliest, attachment figures. As a result, the realistic search for a loved one is frequently sidetracked, swayed, or sometimes brought to a halt by the imbued qualities of one's past and hard-to-release attachments.

After trial and error practice in fantasy, the teen chooses to either progress in social engagement or defensively regress in personal withdrawal. A safe compromise, however unconsciously designed, is to pursue an intimate relationship in its actual form while selecting someone who will match the ministrations offered previously by one or both of the parents. Attraction to a peer of the other gender while simultaneously fearing it is allayed by finding a partner who reinforces one's own ideals as formed in earlier relationship with the opposite-sexed parent.

With frequent occurrence, the adolescent overly defends against his or her fear of attachment and its personal and social consequences by thrusting himself or herself forcefully into a relationship, be it either sexual or platonic in nature. The sudden attachment is then misguided and superfluous, resulting in the teen's fear of being absorbed by the intensity of the passion.

The adolescent pushes himself with honorable intentions into a "crush." The target of the crush is then imbued by the teen with the intended capacity to fulfill the left-over wishes and needs of childhood. Puppy love comprises a first and small, yet significant, step in taking interest in another who is very much alike in personality, interest, and value, and who holds promise for safely finding someone who is compatible. Selecting a partner who mirrors oneself is not only a safe beginning, but also affirms one's own identity. In any case, first intimacies by lovesick, yearning teens are indulged, in great part, for fun and experimentation. Though as blissful and enrapturing as they often are, their expressions are designed for self-support and enhancement. This is both healthy and appropriate for the teenager because the relationship is reciprocal and both partners test their intimate desires.

Adolescent crushes and transient relationships may take a different form, however. The teenager struggles to transform his identity and establish and conduct a cohesive sense of self. He searches for identity catalysts in other persons like family, peers, teachers, and coaches. Personality traits and talents of others admired by the incomplete teen encourage him or her to emulate or study the desired traits. In an intimate relationship, the boy or girl who feels certain elements are missing in his or her identity moves closer to a partner who is deemed to possess these components.

The personality characteristics most admired tend to be the more overt and obvious ones of intelligence, sociability, humor, kindness, gentleness, and charm, However, at a deeper level, what the adolescent looks for in others and wishes to own in himself or herself are the more intrinsic and personal components such as values, ideals, morals, and esteem. Newly acquired self-components aid in the amelioration of loneliness, emptiness, and despair that are so frequently experienced by adolescents in the normal process of development. The reward for this type of relationship is that both partners, as transient as these alliances tend to be, walk away from one another having increased their capacity for self-observation, having received support and empathy from a significant other, having secured a higher self-esteem, and having formed a more cohesive sense of self.

Intimate attachments of adolescence tend to be short lived and superficial, though often emotionally intense. The ego is both vulnerable and gullable during this time, yet biological and social determinants thrust the teen forward into maturity with varying degrees of success. Even in the healthy scheme of personal progression, tendencies to mentally regress to previous states of warmth, comfort, and security in the mother's womb and her loving arms are normal. Fearing dissolution of the self at the lack of mature expression of his or her innate need to love and be loved, the teen may display not only negativism, defiance, and repudiative behavior, but may be inclined toward sudden and unpredictable changes in intimate partners. In adolescent relationships each partner brings to the fore certain unresolved conflicts concerning the parents, eliciting emotions about his or her unfulfilled needs and desires. Resultingly, emotional regression produces anxiety for the teen regardless of whether the return is one of displeasure and unfulfillment, or one of comfort. Hence, the teenager may find even the healthy, satisfying relationships to be psychologically overwhelming and seek flight from attachment. Movement towards the unknown of adulthood is intimidating, and teens may reach for adult like attachments in optimal doses, and in one relationship encounter at a time. While this is not the only healthy means to love, intimacy, and attachment, it is one that is effective and typical of the adolescent experience.

Moral constraints persistently remind the adolescent that it is time to dismiss any lingering, intimate desires for the parents from the oedipal years. Simultaneously, the teen's conscience believes it to be not only acceptable but desirable to find an alternative type of intimate expression in adult sexuality. The ego, in time, comes to view peers of both genders as contemporaries and not reflections of his or her parents. With a healthy dose of optimism and self-esteem, the teen acquires the will to actively yearn for adult gratification and comes to believe there is a place for him or her in both love and the adult world in general.[16]

It is the teen's conscience in conjunction with his strengthening ego that dictates his choice of partner. Having sex or not, the teen's desire is for intimate attachment that will permit mutual experimentation wherein neither partner is ridiculed, exploited, or impinged on.

As a teenager changes attachments he necessarily experiences the pain of emotional loss and is faced with the mourning process. He not only loses the intimate partner, he also loses a part of himself. Each loss is a blow to his ego and lowers his self-esteem. Yet , in the healthy scheme, each loss also encourages a revision of his self-perception, identity, and sexual restriction. As expected, the adolescent's personal esteem rises quickly again at the start of his next relationship. In fact, overall improvement of self-esteem is nourished by a shifting of emotional attention to and from himself in relationship with another. As the teen loses an intimacy with a contemporary, he reinvests his emotions in himself, refueling his depleted self-esteem and providing a base for personal reintegration. The losing and gaining of attachment services the vulnerable teen well by inducing healthy, small vacillations in progression and regression with an overall movement in favor of gradual advancement toward placement in the adult world of mature sexuality and love.

Ultimately, the adolescent's ability to secure a mature adult relationship requires an effective transformation of narcissistic investment in himself to a comparable, emotional concern for another person. This is painfully difficult to achieve. A functional degree of narcissism serves a person well in the formative years. The process of securing this mature love and intimacy is fraught with anxiety and anguish. Intense emotions from desires for something that in reality may or may not ever come to be may be crushing. Love involves both forfeiture and acquisition. The finding of love requires relinquishing a part of the self that must be offered to the loved one. The hope of securing the bliss of unification in meld with the object of one's desire is tempered by the realization that despair is around the corner should the relationship falter. Indeed, the integrity of one's sense of self hangs delicately on the thread of hope. Yet, hope is a precarious state for the vulnerable teen. Idealization siphons a great deal of libidinal energy from a teenager whose ego is already somewhat depleted. Indeed, the teenager is lovesick, and this holds the potential for danger.

Whatever emotional assaults the adolescent may endure, he or she typically survives without catastrophe. The end result of the teen's persistence is the formation of a healthy identification with the other gender. An idealized view of the loved one is integrated with a realistic perception of that person as individualized in his or her own right. Idealization of the self coalesces with idealization of the other in the context of mutual identification of a highly personalized, self- and other enhancing, reciprocation of appreciation, respect, confirmation, and affirmation.

Both partners stabilize and accentuate their gender identities in recognition of both personal and sexual ideals. Sexual expression comes naturally for the adolescent who is able to integrate perceptions of his or her own body with the perception of the partner's genitalia into an organized whole that neatly creates and begs for intimate union and gratification.[17] As each partner is willing and able to come to terms with an appreciation for the other gender, a nonconflicted unification is fertilized and the intimate teenagers can feel and express their sexuality and love to one another without fear of being engulfed by the other. Society and its contingencies contribute significantly to the identity of the teen by providing additional ideals, values, and goals, as well as restrictions. He is accepted by society and, in reciprocation, the late adolescent or young adult gratefully accepts his society and culture as promoters of his personhood and he commits himself to be an integral and supporting member.[18]

The wishes for a blissful reunion with the mother do not cease for the mature, late adolescent and adult. Rather, they express themselves, however unconsciously, through the achievement of sexual satisfaction. The achievement of orgasm, free of conflict and anxiety, requires the ability to contain the intense feelings of immediate excitement, and the ability to lose a bit of one's objectivity in both the course of sex and in the nature of the love relationship.

For the young adult male, in particular, mature love and sexuality necessitate two accomplishments. First, he must be able to fuse his drives for sexual gratification and his gentle tenderness into an offering of intimacy with a female. Sex no longer serves only biological relief and pleasure. Secondly, and resultingly, mature sexuality requires a degree of acceptance of passivity. The young adult male passively, humbly, and gratefully accepts himself as he succumbs to the wonderful pleasures offered by his female partner.

The young adult female experiences mature sexual love as the culmination of a number of lines of personal and social development. By associating with female peers, extended family members, and teachers, the young woman modifies her perception of femininity. As the young woman's relationship with her mother becomes less idealized, she also experiences an alteration of her maternal ideal. She focuses on what motherhood involves, how motherhood had been during her own childhood experiences, and how it may come to be in her own childrearing future. It is the young woman's ego ideal and maternal ideal that determine her sense of femininity and how it will be expressed in her choice of men.

At the brink of adulthood, the adolescent knows solidly who he or she is, of what gender and sexual preference he or she is, how he or she chooses to manifest that gender identification, and what his or her position is in a global, social and cultural sphere. Ideally, the young man and woman feels comfortable with his or her identity and feels sure of his or her ability to effectively engage the world of people, things, and events. Yet, this, too, comes as no easy task. Even upon completion of adolescence, the adult is still faced with the ultimate fear—dissolution of one's self. One eventually submits to the ultimate inability to comprehend the meaning of one's existence or the world in which he or she lives. As philosophically based as this human dilemma appears, it is at the core of one's very being and is particularly relevant during adolescence and early adulthood.

The adolescent's identity and ego strength are normally contingent on the significant person whom he or she has chosen to idealize, identify with, and integrate into one's self-structure by means of internalization. Because of his timidity and doubt, and at times, shame and humility, the teenager seeks these supportive self-extensions as persons who he believes, or fantasizes, will fill the felt void or incompleteness within. They also help him overcome specific disappointments he faces with the reality of parental failures. The periodic and intense feelings of inferiority inherent in the adolescent experience are based on the perceived shortfall from the person he believes he should be upon reaching adulthood. The teen collects images of maturity, sophistication, strength, intelligence, and glamour to guide him in his pending adulthood. Though these qualities seem attainable, he may often see himself as childlike, backward, weak, ineffective, and ugly. The adolescent is psychologically driven toward adulthood, but may feel trapped between childhood and adulthood.

The adolescent is coldly aware that he is left to contend with responsibility, accountability, and functionability all on his own. As he liberates himself from parental ties, and eventually peer ties, the teen experiences a disquieting sense of loneliness. As is true with any loss in the human realm, one adapts by internalizing the lost loved one into one's self-structure, and thereby transforming into an ultimately stronger, wiser, and even more effective person. It becomes the task, then, for the eager teen to seek fulfillment and completion in warm, loving, intimate attachment to another person.

That with which the young adult identifies in the parents is the significant fact that they are sexually active persons. In identification, the young man and woman has a model from which to draw an image and perception of what it means to be a sexually responsible and mature adult. Additionally, the aspiring young adult believes he or she has earned the right to finally engage the adult world as a sexually mature adult. Here the young man and woman must prove his or her effectiveness with the reality of social demands.

Within the context of mature love, intimacy, and attachment, the adventurous young man and woman have created a personal sense of hope, faith, and ambition. Motivated by an unprecedented enthusiasm and inspiration, he or she pursues the ultimate goal—to love and be loved in precious and living memory of the primacy of one's life.

Chapter Eight

Falling in Love

Crossing the threshold into the adult world of love, intimacy, and attachment along with all of the social responsibilities of work, play, and community participation, marks a developmental milestone for both the young woman and man. Having heard the call of maturity, doubting one's own ability to meet the challenge, and having experienced a certain fear of its arrival, the late adolescent enters the arena of adult participation with its attending rewards. Not the least of which, and perhaps the grandest, is the recapturing of the feelings from the primacy of love in current mature sexuality. The enchantment with and devotion to one's chosen partner marks the essence of adulthood, from which further springs all other adult pursuits. Adulthood has begun, and with it is a modicum of fear and helplessness.

That which young adults fear, and in face of which they feel uncertain and at times overwhelmed, is the dissolution of the primary unison and harmony that was blissfully experienced in infancy and so ambivalently relinquished during toddlerhood and later again in adolescence. Although the security and love felt may seem so long ago for the young adult, the emotional contagion is in fact never lost. The young adult may be apprehensive leaving childhood behind, losing ties to the supreme love of his or her origin. After all, isn't this what adulthood is all about? Isn't this the price one pays for adulthood? Actually, no. The love of one's primary experience is yet to be recaptured, indeed recreated, in the form of one's attachment to a contemporary—to one's chosen object of desire, commitment, and mature love.

When a mother gazes into the eyes of her beloved infant she encounters the ultimate expression of maturity and the ultimate sense of reality, reintroducing the love, intimacy, and attachment of her origin. Maturity ushers in for all adults the experiencing of primary love with new color, shading, meaning, and potency. A certain degree of helplessness invades the otherwise wonderful feelings of adulthood. The resurgence of the helplessness felt in infancy during the mother's periodic absences continues in memory trace. Helplessness reemerges with the advent of adulthood because of the inherent responsibilities and expectations that are both personally and socially dictated. As the infant encounters separations in optimal doses from its mother, it begins to recognize the nonself—the person of the mother. This serving of reality instills the feeling of helplessness. The young adult, now severed from the mother under the aegis of maturity, wants nothing more than to recapture the unison's offering of comfort and security.

Adult life mandates a series of accomplishments and acquisitions. They occur not by superceding those of the previous developmental step, rather they are a culmination of all preceding experiences. Each experience is not an isolated event. The person whom one is today and what one searches for in wish fulfilling fantasy and activity is based in its purest form on the infantile experience of mutuality with one's loving mother. Primary love is, and forever will be, the essential and elemental core of who one is.

In all the security and personal containment of the infant experience, it is not surprising a person would not only wish for, but actively seek that comfort in others. While the new adventures of the young adult's new world include work, play, education, and social and cultural involvement, the most important is love. In a mature relationship of intimacy and attachment, the young adult actively strives to assure that there is indeed that one person who wholly has the power to fulfill his or her deepest and fullest wishes. To be satisfied is to recapture the unified, harmonious pleasure of the mother-infant contagion in the form of the mature sexuality and commitment with a partner of one's choice.

When the young adult falls in love, he or she draws upon his or her infantile memory traces of both perfection and disillusionment with the mothering figure that have been laid down as mental engrams and serve as images from which libidinal desires are drawn. Infantile prototypes of the idealized mother and the idealized self in loving meld remain within the unconscious and direct one to fall in love with another who will, in unconscious fantasy, match the prototype. The infantile prototype of perfection, in all realms of experience, is what generates one's search for new love, including adult love.[1]

More specifically, what the young adult strives for is the attainment of pleasure in intimate encounters with a loving partner. Given that the notion of perfection falters during infancy, the person will forever yearn for an attachment that will compensate for the deficits of early life, repair the damage felt, and claim the ultimate feelings of pleasure and fulfillment. Quite simply, all persons traverse the path of life with wounded hearts, and they all desire to have someone who holds promise for healing the wound.[2] Falling in love is much more than simply being in intimate adoration of a chosen lover. It involves a reunion with the idealized mother in all of her love and presence. It is his or her reparative qualities that make the current loved one both loving and lovable.

Falling in love is a condition of the ego, or the sense of self. It is a state in which the ego or self feels complete and whole, reminiscent of the narcissistic state of perfection born from the residues of early memory traces of primary love. Falling in love is, in effect, a temporary and fantasied attempt at mostly an unconscious level to deny both the pain and fear of separateness from the primary figure.[3] The "fall" of the ego in love is actually a regression to an earlier and more primitive, albeit more pleasurable, ego state of existence. The ego inflates as one falls in love, inspite of love's rather simple nature, as it blends in splendor with the ego of the loved one. Falling in love totally absorbs the lover's ego. Hence, the ecstasy felt from truly falling in love.

Conscious awareness of the similarity between the original love of one's mother and the new love figure is minimal, if any. But the old and new loves are synonymous. As was experienced in the mother-infant attachment, both adult persons feel exalted and elated in their ability to feel at one with one another. This is expressed principally with bodily embrace and eye to eye contact, hence, the entrancing experience of "love at first sight." As fantasy based as love at first sight is, its existence and potency are undeniable. There is an inextricable tie between the love of primacy and the adult love at first sight.

The young adult yearns for and seeks a pleasurable life. Naturally, the first and foremost in desire, however it is to be achieved, is to love and be loved. If adulthood is to be perceived as the apex of advancement, it must be represented by something mostly, if not wholly, beautiful and pleasurable. That which holds promise for gratification is the declaration of love. In a healthy, typical sense, the young adult begs for this love. The amorous youth is primed for being in love, and even more rapturously, falling in love.

Unconsciously generated is the magnetism that sparks the adult's fall into love. Just as a baby experiences primary love as it assimilates the entirety of mother's loving and inviting face, so does the adult, especially during youth, respond to the facial expressions of the person with whom he or she falls in love. When eyes meet, an emotional embrace is formed and the future lovers are entranced. The bliss of the mother-infant experience is revitalized. Each lovesick partner recaptures the pristine experience of primary love at the very moment of eye contact. The totality of the alluring goodness of the face is what triggers and crystallizes the fall into love, gives the fall its meaning, and provides the fall its potency. The natural play, and flow, and rhythm between an infant and its mother pronounces in beautiful harmony the fantasy and subjectivity of both adult participants. Each recognizes emotionally, in mutual eye contact, the emerging image of the good mother in all her loveliness.

A feeling of unison is encountered when one falls in love. This subjective state is based solidly on the relationship phenomenon of identification. Identification is the means by which the young child, having clearly acquired the conceptual capacity to recognize himself or herself as a separate and distinct person from the person of the loving and beloved mother, acquires a further capacity to empathize with mother in all her generous ways. Two young adults in the throes of empassioned embrace identify with one another in each partner's capacity and promise for providing the love and intimacy for which all healthy adults strive. The ability to empathize with the goodness of mother, as seen in the potential goodness of the chosen partner as well as oneself, is precisely what fosters falling into love. Each partner seeks the goodliness, nurturance, and presence of eternal warmth and security in the newly discovered person. The foundation is set for a prospectively good fit for the aspiring lovers whose expression of intimacy and attachment reinstates the origin of one's existence.

An identification is not formed with the partner in his or her totality. Rather, a specific aspect of his or her personality is selected and identified with. The characteristic can be one of various qualities that constitute the beloved's personality, and as well, one or both parents' personalities. This is a quality that is cherished in its ability to have brought comfort and pleasure during childhood. The quality sought in the prospective partner may be the one that the adult has deemed missing from his or her relationship with the mother or father. He or she wishes to capture and hold what he or she sadly, yet hopefully, perceives as able to fill the void within.[4]

The identification process varies from person to person, and reflects significantly where each person is in his or her line of maturational progression. The wishes and needs of each person fluctuate along the timeline and context of one's current position in life. Additionally, the person's search for a partner is based not only on a desire for intimacy, but also to protect himself or herself from reacquiring and reenacting painful past relationships with the parents who are perceived to have failed him or her in some capacity.

Seeking a romantic partner and falling in love do not stem solely from an unconscious motivation. At an acutely conscious level of awareness, the young adult yearns for progressive movement toward the future and the promise of both the challenge and joy that it entails. When a young couple falls in love, the event becomes an intricate and interesting blend of conscious and unconscious, progressive and regressive factors. On a purely conscious level, the desire for a partner is guided by the wish to fulfill healthy, personal aspirations of marriage, family, career, hobbies, civic commitment, and so on.

When a young adult pledges commitment to a partner, this commitment holds promise for a certain lifestyle and life plan to which the lovers are equally and compatibly consigned. Each forms a reality based fantasy of what a relationship with the other will hold currently and for the future.

To establish a sense of purpose in the present and to secure a hope for the future, the young adult requires an intense emotional investment in not only the goals and ideals for himself but for another person. The person loved is a person based partly in reality , partly in fantasy, and greatly in the promise he or she holds for helping meet one's personal aims. A love identified by the mere good feeling of being in love is a love misdirected, immature, and doomed to distraction. In contrast, the loved one's purpose and potential is ideally to serve the goal of enrichment of oneself and of the intimate partnership. The attachment is in service of the partners' egos, individually and collectively.

The desire to pursue a relationship and love another springs significantly from a discontent with oneself.[5] While a young adult's aims are new and yet to be fulfilled, there exists a vague, yet painful sense of personal incompletion and dissention. The young adult's loss of childhood innocence, though typically intellectually unexamined, is nonetheless affectively forceful. The intensity of the pain becomes a catalyst to seek a partner, filling the personally felt void, reestablishing a sense of contentedness, and preventing future loss and emptiness.

Absence of a loved one, either past or present, and the triggered sensation of separation and loss should not dismiss the delight and enhancement of truly being in love with the real person of the lover's real being. The urgency of love stems from the critical and desperate wish to avoid the suffering of a love lost. In this regard, love begets pleasure and security. The absence of love begets anguish, sorrow, and uncertainty.

In the earliest years of life the fragile child creates a mental image of what a good, loving parent is and later rediscovers it in the context of love with an adult contemporary. It is comforting to experience the pleasures of early attachment when they are reinforced and revitalized in a current context of intimate relationships.

A current lover serves to bridge the origin of one's life to the fervent wish in young adulthood to continue its rapture in the form of mature attachment, love, and sexuality. Just as the infant and toddler discover, indeed create, the primary attachment, does the mature adult again make a new discovery and effect a new creation in the form of an adult lover. This is exciting to the young adult in the inspiring discovery of a prospective mate, as well as in the belief that one has no less than created this wonderful person from his or her own imagination and desire. The toddler aged child perceives himself to have conquered the exciting and unexpected universe of the other-than-me world, strengthening and consolidating his burgeoning ego. Likewise, the adult enhances his ego in his continued quest of the now, adult world of plenty. For most mature adults, the prized find is of the both fantasied and actual person with whom to fall in love and mutually experience the ecstasy and security of one's primary relationship. The process of creating this special other is generated by one's sense of curiosity. The adult lover wishes not to simply be presented with a prospective mate or accidently stumble across one, but to have seemingly created by joyous anticipation, hope, and will, the person of one's desire.

When the young adult male or female creates a heterosexual lover, he or she is, in effect, reactivating the yearning for the idealized, oedipal parent of the other gender.[6] While the forbidden threat of actualization is no longer present, falling in love in a sense, unconsciously, captures the love of the other-sexed parent. At a conscious level, however, the young adult perceives himself or herself to have simply fallen in love with an exciting, other person.

Falling in love enhances the awareness of one's sexual being and solidifies one's gender identity. Infatuation with a new lover in a sense expresses one's gender identity as either a female or a male and the ability to identify oneself in relationship with the other gender.[7] The mature adult's identity, nonetheless, is not formulated on a singular recognition of being either female or male. Gender recognition and expression is comprised of both identities. There is no identity in being female or male unless drawn into comparison or contrast with the other. Moreover, one proudly expresses one's femininity or masculinity in relations with the other-sexed partner. This expression is best captured during copulation, the ecstasy of which pronounces one's unique femaleness or maleness. Falling in love crystallizes not only one's sexual identity, but also one's broader identity and personal sense of security.

The longing for a partner with whom to express identities is the impetus for the courtship process. Femininity and masculinity are at two opposite poles and what lies between them is what compels the lovers to investigate in the name of love, intimacy, and attachment. The distance between the two poles spawns the desire to pursue the unknown, come to understand what lies between the needs and desires of the opposite genders, and experiment via courtship.[8] Therewith, the gap closes between the polarities of womanhood and manhood. That which lies at the confluence of the apparent dichotomies is love as it is manifested uniquely by a mature couple.

Courting gives the partners the time needed to understand their mutual suspense, their intensifying love for one another, and their building of a crescendo of their needs, desires, and of course, their apprehension. It is the anxiety and hesitation which finalize the courtship and transform the pair into suitable partners for matrimony, whose feeling of "at oneness" with the other and the affirmation of personal worth and esteem are established. The precariousness of their self-concepts serves to regulate the distance between them during courtship, drawing them closer and away from one another in an awkward, rhythmic juggle that ultimately, if all goes well, ends with true desire, acceptance, and commitment. The intensity of the drama can leave both partners insecure, yet poignantly assured that their courtship induced vigor is what makes their love more meaningful. Love is something that both partners need to work at.

There is at least a modicum of uncertainty and hesitation in falling in love for all people. Partners bridge the polarities of femininity and masculinity and augment the desire to be both active and passive in both progressing and regressing in one's selfhood. This phenomenon is paralleled in conceptualization and emotional experience to the separation and individuation experiences of toddlerhood.

For all people, separation induces anxiety because of fears that the separateness may uncontrollably exceed personal comfort. Persons fear disengaging to the point of losing all human connection resulting in a falling into oblivion and a dissolution of the self. The human being is a social being, innately yearning for human, bodily and emotional contact—a sense of belongingness. The acquisition of mature love is, in regard to the struggles of separation and individuation, an accomplishment, and typically comes with great effort as exemplified by the precariousness, awkwardness, and ambivalence encountered by both partners during courtship.

A common motif of courtship is an oscillating parting and reuniting. The young adult is enraptured by the ecstasy of sexual passion and togetherness, yet haunted by the fear of engulfment. It is the expression of fear, however consciously or unconsciously experienced, that marks the reluctance to commit himself or herself to the relationship. One wishes for fusion while simultaneously fears its regressive, merging force.[9] The couple collusively, though mostly unconsciously, organize in mutual anxiety to choreograph a dance in which the partners create obstacles for themselves and their relationship, sabotage their efforts, and establish distrusting situations, all in justifying the need to pull away from the partnership. Young adult lovers tend to struggle to maintain an optimal distance between one another. The acute partings and reuniting of courtship reflect the internal need to regulate closeness at a level tolerable to each partner.[10]

Just as the toddler aged child needs to reestablish contact with the mother for periodic emotional refueling and stabilization, only to disengage her again in pursuit of the exciting world beyond her, the young adult lover parts from his or her beloved only to return in blissful reunion. This repetitive phenomenon regulates the distance between the partners, assuaging anxiety over being too close, while paradoxically sealing their commitment to one another in the exhilaration afforded by the repeated, passionate reunions. If the courtship goes well, both partners advance to a new maturity of love and attachment as each person pursues autonomy and growth without the undue fear of engulfment. Resultingly, each partner captures a healthy balance of the unified feeling that goes with the state of being in love and the necessity to concomitantly remain differentiated and ego autonomous.

There is much truth in the expression that one cannot love another unless one loves oneself. The two phenomena occur simultaneously and in mutual facilitation. Falling in love with another is an attempt to fall in love with oneself, or more specifically, is an attempt to achieve one's idealized self.[11] It is also an attempt to savor the ideal and to flesh out that ideal. Two adults in love serve as affirming extensions of one anothers' selves, providing emotional support to one another. Each partner loves the other from the positional vantage of oneself. This does not, however, suggest that the loved one serves only as a mirror to the narcissism of the other. As true as this is in part, the actuality of the loving partner cannot be denied. Yet, the bliss of falling in love is partially explained by the exalted feeling of simply being in love and relishing the feeling of loving relatedness. It recaptures the primary love and expresses one's wistfulness for the splendor of unification.

When the young adult falls in love, he encounters the expansion of his idealized self, a welcomed boost to his personal esteem which in turn fuels his capacity and tendency to genuinely love his chosen partner. The partner is the targeted recipient of the lover's libidinal energy. The adult not only libidinizes his beloved, but in the process libidinizes himself and his ego-ideal. It is the idealized self for which one strives in unconscious desire that services mature love and sexuality. The ego-ideal holds promise in wishful fantasy for providing the ultimate in self-regard, self-value, and self-affirmation. In a natural way, love for the self elicits love for something of another, be it a personal belief, a social cause, a personally esteemed goal, or the person of another human being. Falling in love with another is facilitated by the projection of one's idealized self-value, regard, and affirmation into the chosen partner.[12] In unconscious fantasy, the loved one embodies for the lover the ego's unattained characteristics for which it strives and which it always to some degree fails to attain, forever remaining as one's ego-ideal. Love, hopefully, partially fills the gap between the ego and its ideal and reinstates the ego's precarious narcissistic balance.

It may appear that the chosen partner simply takes the place of the lover's ego-ideal and that the lover resultingly places love and regard for oneself into the loved one. The partner is then admired for what he or she possesses. If the lover cannot attain the ideal for and within himself, he settles for acquiring it vicariously through the loved one. Yet, this comprises only a partial explanation for the mutual exaltation experienced in the relationship, as well as the overestimation of and infatuation with the respective egos. The lover is not emptied of self-love as he bestows his partner with all that is wonderful and perfect. Self-love and the love of another are paralleled in development and experience. It is the real love between two adults that is the vehicle in which they come to terms with who they are individually and collectively. As it is in early life, in adulthood, the closing of the gap between oneself and one's ideal self is experienced as potent illusion of satisfaction and gratification. It is no wonder that falling in love is so beautiful in a fantastic sort of way.

A substantial price is nonetheless paid for falling in love. The young adult struggled during adolescence to progress in a forward movement with the ultimate wish for and goal of securing the maturity of the adult ego. Regressive pulls had to be self-modulated, attenuated, and at times, vehemently fought against. Yet, to experience the ecstasy of primary love during adulthood requires both the ability and willingness, at both a conscious and unconscious level, to regress.[13] Ego regression is characterized by the forfeiture of a significant part of one's narcissism and personal sense of strength, stability, and security. The lover feels depleted, weak, vulnerable, and humble. Shifting investment of the libido from oneself to another empties the ego of vital substance, leaving the self in deprivation. Testimony reveals the subjective experience of humility by those who take the plunge into love. Self-regard simply diminishes as the lover feels an impoverishment of personal resources. Moreover, personal value is minimized in favor of idealizing and aggrandizing the chosen partner, resulting in an overwhelming sense of vulnerability. The ego regresses and the lover is rendered dependent, weakened, and despaired. Yet, not all is lost, for there does remain a hope for reclamation and the reestablishment of personal substance and integrity.

Hope lies squarely at will. The young adult does not simply fall into the depths of love. Falling in love is motivated by choice, however precariously conscious the volition may be. The young adult falls in love because nature invites it. And in purely economic terms, one falls in love because of the potential for great payoff. There is realistic hope that the partner will return love in like fashion, thereby replenishing the lover's emptied ego. The ego is hence refueled for progressive movement into a new plane of mature love, intimacy, and adult attachment. The newly created self is exalted. No doubt, being loved feels great. Loving and being loved nourish the hearts of two venturous souls.

The vulnerability of falling in love is certain. Unconsciously, the lover sacrifices his personal stability and ego integrity as he acquiesces in idealistically bestowed reverence to the partner. The self of the lover is wide open to injury, for there is no guarantee that one's expressed love will be reciprocated. The lover remains humble until the love is returned and a narcissistic balance is restored. Resultingly, the lover's personal esteem is heightened, the self is enriched, the ego is matured, and the glory of the primal state is recaptured. Primary love is where love for the self and love for the other are indistinguishable. They are one and the same.

Falling in love does not involve a simple decrease in self-regard and self-appreciation in favor of libidinizing the lover. Romance during the courtship permits a healthy interchange of the partners' ideal selves. Resultingly, each partner acquires an understanding of the other's nature as an anticipation of his or her behavior in the future of the relationship. A realistic understanding of his or her own role in the romantic partnership also develops.

The adult lover's idealization of the beloved is a natural and healthy component of attachment formation, and it serves as a preliminary step toward the eventual permanence and mutuality of a mature, intimate relationship. Indeed, idealization is a precursor of the capacity to fall in love.[14] Yet, it is not synonymous with the process of falling in love. The couple in idealized form constitutes a perfect relationship wherein both partners exist in a pure exchange of unalloyed contentedness. But this type of relationship does not exist in reality. It happens only in fantasy, and fantasy is the vehicle that human beings resort to in hopeful compromise for the unconditional fruit of primary love.

The conscious and mutual choices of the partnership are expressed in both the nature and quality of the courtship. To what extent partners fall in love and consummate their attachment is greatly influenced by the actual relationship between the two. While it is significant that each lover during the courtship moves closer to his or her ego-ideal, the two lovers also draw nearer as they manage to avoid the shadings and colorings of their unconscious. The partners move closer to one another, creating a unique kinship and feeling as though they have become much like one another. A joint identification is secured. In the finding of a loved one, the lover finds oneself, credits oneself, and validates oneself. An added perk is the ecstatic feeling of being loved by one so much admired, and viewing himself or herself as deserving of that love.

Falling in love inherently involves a loosening of one's reality sense. Idealization is a defense mechanism employed by a vulnerable ego struggling to avoid its depletion. The young adult yearning for attachment and intimacy is offering himself or herself personally, wholly, and honestly to another person. Weakened by humility and self-depreciation, however, his or her fragile and uncertain self succumbs to defensiveness. The perception of the idealized lover is often phantasmagoric.

Reality testing is suspended in favor of viewing the loved one in idealized form. However, as the courtship proceeds, reality reestablishes itself and the lover comes to accurately perceive the partner. Yet, how quickly and to what degree reality reinstates varies notably from person to person. Some lovers cling tenaciously to their idealized creations, while others are faced solidly with the reality of their partners. The latter often leads to an early disengagement from the relationship. In the healthy process, this is particularly true when the love is unrequited. When love is not reciprocated, the idealization is acutely breached and often becomes painful. But reality's coldness is confronted, the ego is reaffirmed, and the search for the perfect mate starts anew.

The mature adult idealizes his desired partner in a relationship context of empathy, concern, identification, and a corollary desire to comfort the beloved and repair all that is subjectively felt by the beloved to be injured. This healthy form of idealization runs parallel to the healthy experience of falling in love. It is not the more overt aspects of the partner's being that are desired, such as body style, sense of humor, social status, sexual prowess, or the like. A person's idealization transcends these superficial elements to reach the partner's inner core. Those characteristics that are healthily idealized by the mature lover pertain to that which the chosen partner represents in values, ideals, goals, and beliefs.

Magically, it seems, one falls in love. There is something enchanting about seeing something in a partner that has never been seen in a person before. Also, the young lover's sense of self is enriched. It is not only what is seen in the beloved that is so full of wonder, but also the untapped personal resources within oneself that amaze and delight the lover. The power of the intimate attachment lends the lover to believe that perhaps, after all, he has always been the person who has otherwise seemingly mysteriously and surprisingly surfaced during the courtship. Humbly, the adult lover views himself in a new light as a person of charm, interest, appeal, sensitivity, and generosity, etc. Proudly, he claims and professes these newly discovered characteristics, owns them, and maintains them, forever.

Love is not simply a manifestation of biological drive toward genital pleasure and reproduction of the species. The human organism is a social being, embedded in a relational context of other beings. The potency of primary love testifies to the innate desire to secure intimacy with another person, to hold dearly to the attachment and protect it from destruction or subversion.

When falling in love, the adult regresses to an earlier stage of development wherein social relatedness is not yet separated in function from the gratification of needs. Very early in life the child engages the gratifying mother for the ministrations she offers. Likewise, the adult libidinizes his chosen partner for the purpose of need satisfaction. Of course, the adult's needs and desires are maturationally advanced, including the yearnings for bodily contact, genital stimulation, a sense of belongingness, a sense of personal commitment, and a sense of confirmation and affirmation. Yet, these acquisitions are founded no less on a basic gratification of human needs than is the newborn gratefully suckling at its mother's breast. The adult fears his own impoverishment and depletion, and despairs losing the loved one by either abandonment or destruction. This fear generates the tendency to overly esteem the partner and imbue him or her with the undeniable and unquestionable powers reminiscent of the all-gratifying, perfect mother.

A vital aspect of healthy ego functioning tests itself in coitus. During sexual intercourse, and especially at the reach of orgasm, lovers psychologically merge and their libidinal and aggressive impulses are simultaneously released. One's sense of himself or herself as a distinct entity is temporarily suspended as both partners meld. The ecstasy of orgasm reclaims the lovers' primary experiences of love, intimacy, and attachment.

Healthy self-development is required to sustain the short lived, yet powerful, regressions to an undifferentiated state. A lover's sense of wholeness is temporarily lost, constituting a price paid for the rapture of sexual climax. Lovemaking evokes memory traces of earlier experienced, fantasied and illusory engulfment by the original loved one. To the extent that the healthy adult lover can endure the transient loss of one's essential being, he will enjoy the rewards of the return to adult subsistence, to the base of a reality sense, and above all, a transcendence of oneself in the course of coitus and orgasm. An intimate identification is formed with the partner. Resultingly, the lover surrenders in small dosages the security sought at an unconscious level in the primary experience in unison with the good mother. In replacement, the mature lover claims a new relationship in which he affirms himself as a person of autonomy and distinction in identity. The current world of a healthy adult love relationship does not supplant the primacy of one's life. Rather, it superimposes on, expands, and enhances the experience of early, primary love.

The intensity of sexual passion and orgastic pleasure is paradoxically both a progression in ego function and a regression in ego state. Reaching orgasm in the height of ecstasy is born from and reinforces the passion. A lover may relish the opportunity to lose himself or herself in the surrealism of lovemaking and live out the fantasied illusion of imperishability, immortality, and everlasting renewal of one's primary experience.

Passion is a feeling state in which the lover is permitted to cross the border into another realm of oneself. Permission is granted, temporarily, to express primitive sexual urges without fear of reprisal from society, one's partner, or even from oneself. Perhaps the height of passion is vivified by the grand experience of being in love. Falling in love not only elicits the ultimate passion but also the encounter of a sense of novelty and suspense—a begging for curiosity. When one falls in love, an adventure begins and the courtship is likely to be filled with twists and turns. It is a stage of discovery in which the lover is always at surprise, oftentimes enchantment, and sometimes in agonizing conflict. Falling in love is a typically unique experience of intoxicating joy, ecstasy, and inspiration.

However tumultuous the passion of falling in love may be, it acquires its energy from passion's very sense of irrationality. The nonsensical element of passion is what affords the courtship its novelty and begs the lover to pass into the unknown. The entire experience of being in love can be reduced to one certain element. For the healthy individual, falling in love is self-gratifying. It simply makes a person feel good. Falling in love is a narcissistic pursuit. Feeling good about oneself is the reward for love's challenging and sometimes treacherous pursuit.

Falling in love is identified by its reciprocity. The nature of any loving relationship is highlighted by the circular exchange of giving and receiving as an ongoing process. The movements of these transactions are such that there is no determination of where the cycle begins and ends. Surprisingly, the young adult lover cannot and does not distinguish between the love he showers upon his partner and the love that he receives. The circular flow of intimacy, as in the mother-infant dyad, creates a closed, yet internally fluid, active, and self-perpetuating system of give and take. One loves in anticipation of love in return.

A healthy partnership requires the experience of relatedness. Even in the heat of sexual passion when it appears as though the two egos have abated in deference to their instinctually driven ids, the egos still retain supremacy. At the height of passion between lovers it is not only the biological urges of instinct that are satisfied. The ego of each partner strengthens and expands with pride and integrity, as well. The two lovers feel great about themselves and one another. Intensity of passion does not stifle or contradict the promulgation of their two egos. Two ids on fire, as long as the egos monitor and contain the instinctual drives, serve to strengthen the egos and their relatedness.

Additionally, sexual passion, while servicing temporarily a biological impulse, in a long term sense, aids in the development of empathy and genuine concern for the partner. At the height of sexual climax is also the height of mutual identification as each partner temporarily loses himself or herself in the person of the loving partner. This permits the egos to lose and regain their equilibrium in tolerable doses. Egos maintain the required ability to master the instinctual drives. Sexual passion does not mitigate a healthy love founded on mutual empathy and concern. It augments the real and fantasied adoration held by one's partner, fostering the desire to partake in the other's radiance.

The nature of relatedness is vague in conceptualization. It is elusive to any and all who investigate it. This is why falling in love is characterized by expressed cliches that only mystify and simplify the experience. Love's ways are merely bestowed upon us by something that perhaps we are not meant to understand, lest one spoils it all. We dare not conceptually diminish love by considering it a purely biological phenomenon. Love may, but then may not, have anything to do with sex. Sex and love integrate well in mutual experience and expression, but they are not synonymous. The ability to copulate is a biological and physiological given to the medically healthy adolescent and adult. But it is little more than that. Neither does sexuality and its manifestation need to be learned. Nature takes it course. If sexual activity and reproduction are experienced under the aegis of love, intimacy, and attachment, this constitutes a wonderful phenomenon. But it does not come naturally. Love is an experience that must be expressed early in life, nurtured, protected, and cherished. When love occurs during the primacy of one's life it will continue to be promoted, never to expire.

Chapter Nine

The Mature Love and Sexuality of Adulthood

There remains one component of love that begs investigation. How does one go about selecting a mate? Or, how is it that the selection of a mate just seems to happen? As noted in chapter eight, a lover seeks his or her own ego-ideal in a partner. The realistic evaluation of a prospective mate, of which the lover is consciously aware, comes into confluence with unconscious motivations based on repressed needs, wishes, and fantasies. It is this admixture of the known and the unknown, the desired and the feared, that creates the mystery and challenge of mate selection. The lover who seeks reality based characteristics in a mate is considered rational, careful, and pragmatic. However, some question the genuineness of this love. Should a mate be selected by comparison shopping as one would purchase an automobile?

The aspiring lover who assesses a potential partner as one would interview a prospective partner in business will note characteristics such as physical beauty, intelligence, sociability, and financial stability. While these qualities may well be desirable, they may not coincide with one's ego-ideal, for the nature of the ideal self is unconscious to the lover. Unless a person undergoes psychoanalysis, he is unlikely to understand or articulate his ideal. One argument might be that the selection of a mate is strictly determined by the unconscious if it is to meet one's ideal and therewith be of true love. A green, two door coupe, for example, may appeal to a person at a conscious level. But unconsciously, that automobile may represent symbolically something much more personal, esteemed, and indeed, much more unknown to its admirer. This latter constituent is what makes the driver fall in love with the automobile. In analogy, an aspiring lover falls in love with another for reasons that are unknown to him. The unconscious component of mate selection and courtship is what provides the prospective mate his or her appeal.[1] This truism explains that to fall into the depths of true love, one must feel the pangs of longing and feel the despair at the thought of not capturing the other's heart. Love comes at a price.

Perception is one of many ego functions that occurs within the realm of conscious awareness. In the normative process, the human ego perceives the reality of a person, thing, or event. Yet, the unconscious dimension of falling in love overshadows this reality testing function, as the adult tends to locate a partner undiscerningly and without clarity. Hence, love is blind. The ego is vulnerable in its ability to accurately observe the true qualities of the loved one and assess the likelihood of an honest relationship. While some sense of reality is required to accurately evaluate the possibility of lifelong love, instinctual wishes mitigate the ego's judgment. Harm incurs if the lover becomes hypersensitive to or welcomes misleading signs that a love is requited, when in fact, the feelings are not reciprocated. Likewise, motivation may be clouded by a purely conscious desire to have and keep a love simply because it is viewed, and perhaps proven, to be difficult to attain. A love misdirected is a love that may be motivated purely by the challenge of the obstacle. True and honest love does present obstacles intricately defined by the respective personalities of the two partners, even when the two are genuinely and healthily attracted to one another.

Natural and inevitable obstacles to a successful courtship are born from the unconscious directives of the lovers in relational concert, if not in collusion, as well as the reality based disagreements and dissentions that exist between the two partners.[2] It is fact that falling and remaining in love are not merely or solely the result of unconscious factors. Lovers do choose partners based on practical and functional purposes, as well. The chosen partner's characteristics that attribute to the functioning of a workable relationship may be all that is required for a partnership to strike and thrive, however limited in or devoid of true love. Such a relationship can survive because of its equilibrium, much like a business partnership. It can be a very healthy and workable relationship.

There is no doubt, however, that choosing a companion with whom to fall in love, as rapturous as the relationship may or may not be, is determined by the conscriptive prototypes of the primary love relationship. The earliest experiences of loving and blissful engagement still provide the lovers with the emotional and relational blueprint from which they direct their courtship and their unique encounter with love.

But it isn't only the loving experiences with mother, and later, father, that influence and guide the adult form of love. The guideline for the "perfect" love is, indeed, established and solidified by the engrams laid down in the memory of the infant in the mother-child attachment. But by adulthood, what is sought in a loving partner is a composite of all previous love experiences founded on the prototype. Grandparents, siblings, schoolmates, teachers, coaches, scout troop leaders, and the like, for example, levy a significant impact on one's personhood. What the aspiring adult lover seeks is not simply someone who replicates the mother or the father, but someone who may possess specified traits of a variety of important persons with whom he or she has previously been involved. In essence, it is an amalgamation of characteristics that are the best of what has been experienced, starting with, and always colored by, the loving mother.

As discussed in earlier chapters, an adult lover has maturationally forfeited his intimate involvement with his mother and father, only to recapitulate the security and goodness by attachment to subsequent others. The self-images that love evokes regenerate the original, perfect feeling state. Every bit of love received also leaves its mark on the ego, and it is never lost. Love is renewed and expanded by ongoing, intimate relationships. In this regard, the adult has painfully lost what he once was in the bliss and harmony of primary love. Yet, optimistically, he gains in mature attachment new and enhanced images of himself. These images, comprised of an amalgam of loved and loving persons, inherently command their own respect and dignity. The adult can and does love himself in both his individuality and his participation in loving, intimate attachment with a partner.

A new love should not supplant the endeared and honored persons of the past. On the contrary, the beloved strengthens, substantiates, and validates the lover and all of his or her childhood love relations that were internalized. Because the adult lover has proven his or her capability and propensity to love and be loved, he or she can successfully embark on the mutual gratification of mature love and sexuality.

Even though there is a continuity of the experiences of love incurred during early childhood and adulthood, these experiences are separated in time by the two distinct periods of later childhood and adolescence. If the stages of early childhood and adulthood were immediately successive in time, the intimate nature of the mother-child bond would simply transfer to a comparable relationship in adulthood. The result would be two relatively nascent egos relating to one another with yet an only primitive and archaic sense of separation, differentiation, and individuation. Disaster would be inevitable. By nature's way, the prolonged phases of childhood and adolescence serve the necessary function of nurturing the developing ego's sense of autonomy and self-sufficiency in preparation for adulthood. This same developmental period also affords the child and teenager the needed time and social experiences to confront the pain of letting go of one's primary figures. Cognitive and emotional resolution must be achieved, leaving the youngster's ego aligned with its newly acquiring liberation and autonomy.

A solid ego identity is necessary for adult love and sexuality to form and flourish under the aegis of maturity. Two immature adult egos might successfully participate in a functional relationship if each was interested only in securing the gratification of sexual needs. But the matured emotional structures of the two individuals involved must be able to accommodate more complex needs, desires, and drives. Sexual gratification in the maturity of adulthood is intertwined with happiness and personal fulfillment. The acceptance of, and dependence on, one another provide a sense of assurance that love will sustain through the partners' lives. The love relationship will flourish over time because they can not only tolerate, but welcome the inevitable challenges that any normal relationship encounters. The love felt modifies itself in response to critical events such as parenthood, the "empty-nest" separation, grandparenthood, and retirement. These healthy events provide a challenge to strength and endurance, and test the insolubility and integrity of both the relationship and the individuals' commitment.

The crux of the healthy challenge which the mature love of adulthood delivers is the unavoidable ambivalence that each partner experiences in regard to the other.[3] In a love relationship there is a heightened sense of ambivalence about the partner, and moreover, about oneself in relation to that partner. As the alliance evolves with time, the ambivalence toward oneself and the partner diminishes in favor of a healthy increase of mutuality and interdependence. The reality sense of both partners solidifies as each learns to accurately identify all aspects of the other's entire personality, including the strengths and weaknesses each one possesses. Each lover's autonomy is accepted, allowing for heightened security and confidence in his or her makeup as a masculine or feminine person, and as one who feels good about oneself.

Additionally, what is at the core of one's ambivalent feelings about the other is each partner's perception of the self and how he or she handles issues of dependence and independence, gratification and frustration, instinctual wishes and moral constraints, and love and hatred. These issues remain unresolved for everyone through the course of life. Tolerance of the resulting ambivalence gives testimony to the tenacity of love. True love remains intact only if it is founded on sensitivity, tenderness, empathy, and commitment towards one's lover. Identification with and idealization of the beloved, as they were similarly experienced with the mother, facilitate and energize this enduring phenomenon.

A solid sense of personal identity and personal differentiation allows the mature adult lover to merge with his partner, especially during sexual intercourse, without fear of being engulfed or of dissolution. The mature adult can acknowledge the difference between himself and his lover as persons. The distinction is not only conceptualized, but also appreciated for its allowance of a unique other human with whom to be in love and to share one's personal experience. The beloved other is anointed as the person into whom to project one's own feelings as an intimate means of mutual identification.

A sense of mastery with one's life is perhaps the highest form of personal achievement a human can experience. The acquisition of mastery is related to all aspects of a person's life, and perhaps above all, intimate attachment. Two partners who have each reached this level of mastery have each acquired the confidence in oneself, the other, and the partnership that enables the relationship to solidify intimately.

In order to feel good about oneself, the mature adult lover must acknowledge, accept, and experience his uniquely personal needs. When these needs are met, his autonomy expands. He feels good about both the gratification of his needs and the very existence of those needs. The mature adult is empowered by the acknowledgement that his beloved partner is satisfying. Reciprocally, he feels a sense of achievement in gratifying the needs of his beloved. Partners who are in empathic attunement with one another intuitively respond to one another's needs, and do so with exquisite accuracy. The healthy couple can foresee the needs of the other and discerningly modify their individual needs to accommodate their mutual needs. Performed at both conscious and unconscious levels of awareness, the partners' intent is to maintain the integrity of the unit so that individual needs can be continuously met as the needs of the partnership are satisfied.

The more secure each partner is in the acceptance of his or her selfhood, the more exalting the shared intimacy. Part of the definition of maturity is the capacity and willingness to be intimately close with a contemporary. Maturity, by any definition, involves the capacity for not only intimacy, but also faith in their commitment to permit alternating dependence of one partner on the other. As noted, the ego regresses periodically, permitting the adult lover to merge with the partner in a healthy state of identification. The union, in turn, gives each partner the impetus to thrust forward once again in ego progression, to emphasize and promulgate one's own identity, and paradoxically, to become more differentiated and defined as an adult person among others.

Human beings, by nature, are needful creatures. The need to love and be loved is tantamount to their social being. Unless an intimate attachment in adulthood is founded, nurtured, and cherished, one's needs will not be fully met. Yet, needfulness is a two-way street. Needing and being needed are two sides of the same coin. An intimate adult attachment based on equality of partners is the ideal relational context in which to secure one's own needs and desires. Each partner realizes, however humbly, that he or she must give something of the self in order to receive something of the other. Moreover, each partner must negotiate a change in his or her self in order to secure a reciprocating, cooperative, and adaptive partnership.

While a healthy love relationship serves to meet the needs of the two partners, the healthy adult is nonetheless faced with the fact that not all needs and desires can be fulfilled. As the infant's every need and desire is not and cannot be met by its mother, the sadness experienced at the hands of a partner in an adult relationship that cannot and should not satisfy all desires, parallels in experience.

In the course of a healthy adult relationship based on true intimacy and love, it becomes not only possible, but necessary, to meet one's own needs simultaneous to meeting those of the partner. This is particularly important when it comes to sexual intimacy. As each partner validates his or her bodily self and accepts it for what beauty it possesses and for what interest the chosen partner claims in it, he or she confirms one's desirability and identity as a competent lover. In the process, he or she enhances his or her own self-image while gratifying the sexual longings of the other. They establish a relationship enhancing trust in one another's willingness and ability to sexually excite and be excited, and trust one another physically and emotionally with a degree of gentle, sexual concern and appreciation. Passionate sex and tender love confirm and affirm the self through the intimacy and gratification of the loving and sexual other.

During sexual interplay, the two lovers who accept one another with genuine and mutual empathy, concern, and appreciation intuitively develop an intricate sensitivity to the tastes and distastes of the other. Partners are prepared for the cues and signals of each other and, in the context of desire, welcome the opportunity to please and be pleased. It is often in the bedroom that a couple is first and foremost successful in accomplishing this delicate, yet seemingly easy task. When all goes well, this type of sensitive transaction transcends lovemaking and typifies the totality of the relationship. Matured partners tolerate, support, and encourage one another. They develop a sense of gratitude for the empathy that they receive, the tolerance that is offered, and the commitment which their partner delivers. This is indeed a mutual process, one born from true love and thoughtful acceptance. Gratitude is felt for the beloved not just because of who he or she is as a person, but also for the generosity with which he or she provides support. Nobody in the throes of mature adult love denies that the person that he or she is, is the person that the beloved partner has permitted and promoted him or her to be.

As mutual identification strengthens in the couple, so, too, does a specified identification with one another's sexual desires and propensities. Both genders are able to appreciate the unique femininity or masculinity of the other. Each empathizes with the sexual and otherwise personal needs of the other, facilitating the expression of tenderness in the relationship, especially during lovemaking. The partners are able to feel good about themselves collectively and individually for what the relationship offers. Lovers idealize the relationship, the united partnership, and the commitment thereto formed by both partners. The ideal for which one strives is that of the loving, intimate bond—indeed a promise of commitment to the future of the relationship and its individual membership.

Partners serve as mirrors to one another. Each feels understood and accepted in a way that may not have been previously experienced. There is a strong attachment and a sense that each partner has become what he or she has always wished to be. There is hope that each partner may serve to heal that which feels injured from the past. Genuinely grateful for one another, the couple develops a mutual sense of responsibility for the personal evolution of both partners during the course of the relationship. They share in one another's delight in the changes that take place individually as well as in the relationship itself. Mature love necessitates mature responsibility.

Lovers assume their responsibility individually and collectively as they grow in team effort. There is an inherently shared, common subjectivity that is unique to the intimate dyad. The couple perceives of itself as an encapsulated unit in differentiation from the external world. Normatively, the couple as a unit interfaces regularly with the outside-of-us environment, but the inside-of-us sphere is one of special experience and manifestation. Yet, the couple can be "one" only to the extent that they acknowledge and accept their respectively distinct identities, form an identification with another's individuality, and very importantly, genuinely empathize with one another. In order to fully acknowledge one's partner, one must be able to project one's own subjective experience and personal feelings into the partner. Each lover infuses the other with his or her own emotions and livelihood. And each lover experiences the emotions and perceptions of the other in terms of his or her own emotions and perceptions. This does not create an idiosyncratic distortion of what the other is feeling or thinking. On the contrary, this phenomenon encourages the projecting partner to utilize his or her feelings and thoughts as a way to connect to and reciprocate with those of the beloved. Not only does each partner feel a linkage to the experience of the other, but also forms a link with his or her own experience by empathizing with oneself in that experience and affording oneself the ability to support the self in one's own feelings. To feel good both for and about the beloved partner, the lover must feel good for and about oneself.

The mutual identification that the couple forms also gives them the opportunity to affirm their respective identities. One's identity can only enhance when involved in an attachment as intimate as that of a mature love relationship. Of even more significance is the ability of the two lovers to clarify their individual sexual roles and their contribution to the functioning of the dyad. Certainly more pronounced during sexual interplay, clearly defined sexual roles are also important to the entirety of the relational context, permeating all of the tasks of adulthood including household responsibility and parenthood.

Each partner in the love relationship brings with him or her a solid gender identity. Any healthy intimacy will incorporate the two polarities of femininity and masculinity. However, the relationship will flourish and intensify when the feminine-masculine line of partnership is balanced. Femininity and masculinity compliment one another and help define the mature relationship. They need not and should not be an either-or proposition. The feminine-masculine line that comprises the dyadic unit will be one of a continuum rather than a contribution of the two polarities.

By definition, the human identity is not one of pure femininity or pure masculinity. All humans are constitutionally endowed with both feminine and masculine traits, wishes, fantasies, and instinctual urges. A person, however simply or complexly, is born sexual. Whether the sexual desires are acted on in a feminine or masculine way or in an active or passive way, is of a multifaceted determination. What is clear and concise, however, is the universal fact that all persons are oriented bilaterally toward both feminine and masculine desires and tendencies. What the mature woman brings to a prospectively sound love relationship is a personhood founded solidly on feminine merit, virtue, and passion, yet interspersed with traditionally acknowledged masculine traits, such as, correctly or incorrectly socially determined, strength, proactivity, and aggressiveness. Likewise, the mature man brings to the same relationship his predominantly masculine characteristics intertwined inherently with feminine tendencies, again correctly or incorrectly socially determined, such as self-denial, altruism, sensitivity, and sensuality. While there may well be great diversity among persons concerning their conscious and unconscious propensities, there is a necessary admixture of femininity and masculinity in the relationship.[4]

The degree of feminine and masculine tendencies expressed will vary by person and relationship. Yet, typically, couples match in their accommodation to one another's unique mixture of feminine and masculine components. The strength of the man's feminine wishes and tendencies will usually be equal to the strength of the woman's masculine propensities. This makes for not only easy adaptability in the partnership, but also permits each lover to utilize the other's inclinations to clarify and promote those same inclinations in oneself. Each lover forms an identification with the biologically determined wishes, desires, and fantasies of the other that are counter to his or her own biologically determined proclivities. By identification with the traits of his other-sexed partner, the man vicariously experiences his feminine ways. Conversely, the woman projects her masculine ways into her partner and vicariously lives them out through him. Each partner, then comes to terms with his or her counter-gender characteristics. Each partner affirms and reinforces the biologically determined identity of the other while sensitively supporting the counter-gender components.[5]

Partners of intimacy not only accept, but enhance, one another by clearly delineating and valuing their complete identities inclusive of dual-gender components. Appropriately, both partners solidify and stabilize their respective gender based personalities rather than diffuse their identities in the mix of male-female interplay. Couples vacillate in sexual activity and passivity, femininity and masculinity, dependence and independence, and contribute to the progressive thrust of their individual egos, strengthening their sense of reality and promoting their autonomy and self-sufficiency.

The practice of a clearly and firmly demarcated self-identity includes being in intimate attachment with another, temporarily regressing in fusion with the image of the glorious mother of primacy, and altruistically sacrificing one's personhood and self-regard in favor of the beloved who represents ideally the epitome of perfection. Lovers feel the pangs of intense longing and desire for the one person without whom one believes that one cannot exist, while yet acknowledging that the beloved is not a personal possession and that he or she can fade in a soft beat of the heart. Yet, as has been noted, temporary merger with the self of another human being begs the dire threat of dissolution of one's own self, indeed, the loss of one's identity. The hesitant lover typically acquiesces to his desire and overcomes the dread of engulfment regardless of the strength of his fear of dissolution. What is left at this phenomenal juncture constitutes the very stuff of precisely that which energizes and propels the intensity of love forward. This is passion—the very power of love and lovemaking. Passion acquires its drive from the mystery turned fantasy, turned "heat" that sustains the attachment and gives it its uniquely inspirational flavor.

The passion of love and its expression in sexual interplay stems from the mystery of the forbidden. Couples engage one another in an array of interactions that provide new experiences for both partners and offer no foretelling of the relational outcome. Committed partners brave the unknown, timidly or brazenly, with anticipation of securing for themselves that which is forbidden to them—forbidden knowledge, forbidden experience.[6] Regression to an undifferentiated state of infancy is indeed forbidden. It fuels the fear of dissolution and both defies and decries the progressive push toward autonomy and individuality for which the eager adult had striven so fervently through childhood and adolescence. Nonetheless, the mature, loving adult is enticed by the regressive venture into primary unison with the mother, now disguised as the beloved partner. This experience is forbidden. There are certain shadowings from past experience that one must put to rest, that one must not venture into.

In addition to the forbidden regression to the mother-infant dyad, there is also the taboo of incestuous desires heightened during the oedipal years of three to five or six. After the oedipal resolution the child's sense of morality and conscience confines and then thrusts into repression all desire to usurp the same-sexed parent and secure an exclusive attachment to the opposite-sexed parent to love for one's own. However, as psychoanalysis understands, the repressed tends to return. Repressed oedipal wishes lie dormant in the unconscious during childhood, only to resurge during adolescence and adulthood. The adolescent fervently and frightenedly rejects oedipal longing for the parent of the opposite sex. Later, the adult will yearn for its recapitulation. But because of cultural, social, familial, and moral constraints, the adult embraces the oedipal desires in disguised form. Upon securing a beloved partner based on maturity and commitment, the adult lover has found his or her object of forbidden oedipal longing. The heterosexual partner partially fills the void of the desired parent of the other gender who served as the object of one's early sexual wishes.

The oedipal aged child of three to five or six years, nascent in his conceptual capacity, does not quite understand the nature of his parents' social relationship—that of their marriage. All the child knows is that the parents have something wonderful and powerful and loving, yet untouchable and unknowable. Not only can the child not partake in their special, loving relationship, but he is not to even know it. It is precisely this lack of knowing that induces the adult lover to, after so many years, acquire the knowledge of oedipal desire, to experience it, to savor in its joyful offerings. Adults are free to challenge cultural, social, and personal prohibitions, and may actualize their oedipal desires by sexually capturing the unapproachable parent of the other gender. This experience allows for the passion of adult lovemaking in its most mature form. As previously mentioned, passion stems from involving oneself in something that is forbidden, acquiring knowledge of its existence, and therewith solving its inherent mystery. Mystery is, in essence, the grist for passion. Sexual interplay, including foreplay, coitus, and afterplay, constitutes stages in the solving of the mystery. If the sexual partner is not mysterious, even if only in one's mind, then one is not impassioned. If a couple makes love without at least a vague sense of pursuing something that is taboo, then they are not impassioned. If lovers do not to some degree or in some quality frustrate the forbidden sexual desires of one another, then they, again, are not impassioned. Passion, although more pronounced during sexual intercourse but fashionable in other areas of the mature relationship, is what keeps the attachment alive and secure.[7]

The mystery of intense personal intimacy and breeching the taboo in the context of a mature attachment and a sensitive identification provide for and nourish the fun and the gratification of the relationship. The partnership's longevity may be contingent on the couple's ability and willingness to have fun in bed. The young child acquires the developmental capacity to use objects with which to play. An object is the symbol of something that offers the child pleasure at play in solitude. Later in childhood, the ability to share in the playful experience with another person enables the child to learn more about himself vis-à-vis the playful other. These experiences are the precursor of playfulness in all realms of adulthood. Sexuality, specifically, affords the mature couple the freedom to be creative within the partnership and discover through the mutuality of intimate gratification and identification, their individual and collective selves.[8]

In the blissful merger of coitus and orgasm is paradoxically a strengthening of the perception of the individual identities. The self is of clear distinctiveness, though in a relationship with the self of another. Identification fosters this paradoxical phenomenon. Each partner's gender identity is not only augmented and illuminated, but cherished by both. Each lover graciously and gratefully satisfies the sexual and otherwise intimate desires of the other. Each enjoys gratifying the beloved sexually as much as he or she enjoys being gratified. As the couple during lovemaking learns of what pleases the partner and what pleases oneself, a mutual sexual identification forms. Gratifying and being gratified are one and the same experience and neither partner takes the other for granted. Each partner disquietly acknowledges that the other is a separated individual who can at any time disengage from the partnership. This typically does not happen so long as the couple remain in intimate harmony.

Sexual interplay, particularly during orgasm, provides the only opportunity to experience the fullest height of mutuality. At all other times in the relationship, as healthy as the attachment may well be, there is inherently an element of narcissism that colors the relationship for each partner. In the mature relationship, narcissistic pursuit does not mean self-gratification at the expense of the other, however. On the contrary, seeking pleasure for oneself implies a secure notion that what pleases oneself naturally pleases the other. However, no matter how healthy the partnership is, the desire to balance one's own pleasure with that of the beloved partner, as altruistic as it is, is nonetheless fraught with anxiety for typically both partners. Both are anxious to perform for the other. The man, because of personal, social, and cultural determinants, wishes to express to the woman he loves his sexual prowess, through his virility and potency. This manifestation of both narcissistic and selfless desire to be all of the man he can be can also compliment the best of the woman. Lurking behind every desire, however, is a fear that the desire may not materialize. Also because of personal, social, and cultural elements, the woman may experience fear during lovemaking. In addition to pleasing her man and being the woman who extracts the full masculinity of her partner, she, to some degree, also struggles with the issues of pregnancy, parenthood, family values, and personal integrity. The consequences of sexual intercourse are both more apparent and more serious for the female.[9] This increase in anxiety behooves her to seek the ideal, healthy, mature love with a man who can and will proclaim his commitment to her.

In the course of time, the physical mechanics of sexual intercourse lose their significance in the expression of love. While mutual, physical acumen may be prized by many couples, for most, tenderness, sensuousness, and sensitivity serve as the manifest demonstration of the couple's intimacy and desire. What is of importance to the loving pair is the certain knowledge of commitment, loyalty, and personal integrity. This is accomplished by the couple's intuitively perceptive sense that they possess the capacity to meet their individual and collective needs through the entire realm of their relationship. In alternating fashion, one partner assumes a temporarily passive position, both in a physical and psychological sense, while the other occupies a more active role. One partner submits masochistically to the mildly sadistic needs of the other. Through exhibitionism, one lover generously displays his or her sexual offerings for the voyeuristic consumption of the other. In alternating and respectful interplay, the couple benevolently provides for the sexual desires of one another. The passion thrives and the couple maturely sustains.

Mature sexuality requires a healthy moral structure that promotes a sense of conscience in relating to and loving another person. The superego's guiding morality and conscience permit one to idealize the beloved partner and encourage commitment to the attachment. In childhood, the superego provides love and a feeling of well-being while inhibiting the activation of impulsive urges. In the maturity of adulthood, the superego plays somewhat less of a moralistic, inhibiting role and more of a protective function supporting the integrity of the ego, and the sense of one's self. Part of the protection of the self lies in the superego's allowance for the ego to have and to show empathy for another person, as well as to sexually enjoy the beloved without unduly harsh proscription and inhibition. The conscience encourages healthy sexuality and freedom to sensually explore and experiment with one's sexual fantasies. In adulthood, the function of morality is to protect oneself from excessively punitive guilt and recrimination, including the guilt of sexual desire. Mature adult lovers are free to play with one another without being consumed by the passion.

When the couple reaches the maturational point of complete, unqualified trust and respect in their mutual intimacy, not only do they transcend their individual selves to advance to a higher level of organization in their unified relationship, they rise even beyond the unitary partnership. The couple is at one with society as a whole. In their mature love, they have mystically connected with humanity in all of its meaning and purpose. Now an integral part of all that is defined as the human experience, the couple commits its partnership to the progression of the human race. In the normative process, the young adult couple is acutely aware, however vaguely conceptualized, that it is time to plan for a family. It is time to manifestly express the unique nature and quality of their loving relationship in commitment to the integrity and advancement of humankind. In this regard, there exists a largely personal link between the young couple in love and attachment, and in mankind in global determination. This phenomenon, however conscious or unconscious, crystallizes their adult identities and partnership, while reinforcing their intimate attachment, personal esteem, and contributive value.

Only to the extent that a couple has reached this maturational milestone can they feel a sufficient degree of comfort within their relationship to experience their attachment in privacy. They find it both appropriate and enjoyable to partially withdraw their investment in the greater environment in favor of turning into themselves, enjoying the peace and tranquility of their attachment. Lovers wish to be alone to savor their alliance and also to find their needs met within and by their partnership. They do this by their own reasoning and less so by the dictates or expectations of the society or culture. The couple determines its own narrowly circumscribed set of social goals, ideals, and values, creating their own sense of cultural expectation and morality.

Within the context of a pronounced union, lovers in intimate attachment secure for themselves a unique provenance of their own. Their sacramental union is defined, generated, and nourished by its very existence and perpetuation. Intimation is generated easily, intuitively, and above all nonverbally. Solitude and silence permit the lovers to create for themselves a highly charged, emotional setting wherein each is in fine attunement with his or her own internal sensations. It is in a state of quiescence that the individual can come to terms with his or her own subjectivity. Lovers intricately contribute to the partnership, designing a collective subjectivity of quiet tranquility within which they locate and proclaim their loyalty and commitment, by the very grace of their love.

Chapter Ten

The Loss of a Loved One

Love is neither an acquisition nor a possession. Love, expressed in the context of intimacy and attachment, is both a process and an experience. It is felt by the body from within, capturing the heart, the soul, and the spirit, giving the human being its identity and its reality. Moreover, the experience of love does not have a beginning or an end, for it does not belong to the individual or his or her particular existence. Love's tenancy and heritage is found in the advancement and the sanctity of not only the human being but the human species.

It is acknowledged that love is not an unqualified given. As beautiful and powerful as it is, love can be quickly lost. The sorrow of a lost love, a love so endeared yet so seemingly harshly removed from one's presence can only be described, though not explained, by the person who has experienced it. When a person loses a loved one by death, what has been lost transcends the embodiment of a person so cherished and admired. Gone is not only this person, but also a part of oneself so lovingly attached to the departed. The survivor misses both the beloved other and the aspect of oneself purely identified with the deceased. The process of love may seem to end, though it does not. In actuality it becomes a transformed love held in the heart of the survivor who is issued the task of adaptation. Psychoanalysis refers to this task as "the work of mourning."[1]

As typical of all varieties of work, the anticipated reward is the payoff. But what can conceivably be rewarding about the death of a loved one? At the risk of undermining the significance of the anguish loss causes, it may be suggested that there is compensation for surviving this painful transformation. Death can make those left behind stronger, wiser, and more personally effective than before. How and why a person could benefit so much requires an intricate look into the psychodynamics involved in the mourning process.

The mourning process is unique yet universal to all human beings. The bereaved loses an attachment that had been so preciously formed and so coldly taken away. The survivor's continued love for the departed is based not merely on a person to person relationship, but a loss of oneself, a self having its root of existence in the primacy of one's life. This is a self reflective of the comforts granted by a nurturing mother. It is no wonder that an attachment to someone can transcend the immediate relationship. A loving relationship, at any point in two persons' lives, encompasses both parties' entire maturational development. Understandably, a mourner may be incapable of accepting loss and relinquishing the attachment to the deceased. The cruelness of reality and the significance of the loss initiates the mourning process, the course of time and hard work that will eventually allow the mourner to adapt to a new existence without the deceased. Testimony to the paradoxical nature of human beings, fragile and sensitive yet resilient and irrepressible, most people do adapt and carry on. The prerequisite courage inherent in the work of mourning illuminates the tenacity with which the human clings to one's personal integrity and sustenance in the midst of external and internal onslaught. Change can be difficult, without question, especially when the changes are private, sudden, and unwanted, and can be construed as no less than a personal violation or insult. Yet, it is the very impenetrable love for the departed that generates the mourning process and transforms the self.

Dejected, emptied, and shocked upon the initial knowledge of the loss, the stricken survivor may withdraw into himself or herself, turning away from everything and everybody not connected to the deceased. The outside world may seem frozen in time as the loss and surrounding circumstances are magnified. In time, the survivor adapts to reality's mandate, but the actuality of the loss and its acceptance comes neither quickly nor effortlessly.

The tendency, or in some instances, the desperate need, of the mourner to disavow the loss in his or her immediate world has both a psychological and a biophysiological basis. Internally, the deceased sustains in the mourner's existence. This is beyond a mere memory of the departed. Denial is defensively employed by those not ready to let go, behaving as if the person is still present. In spite of an otherwise acknowledgement of loss, the mourner unconsciously attempts to recover an only momentarily lost or misplaced loved one. It is both difficult and frightening to give up a libidinal relationship established over years, and perhaps decades, of commitment and reverence.

In the course of effective mourning, the attachment is relinquished in optimal doses and in slow yet steady steps as energy is simultaneously directed to other persons, things, and events. The end result is not a "giving up" of the loved one and a "moving on" in other aspects of living. Rather, the accomplishment of effective mourning is a diminution of the drive that originally attached the mourner to the deceased. New sources of gratification and happiness can be found in any number of other significant persons or valued life activities. But the attachment to the lost person never ends, nor is it supplanted by another love. What modifies is the quality of the attachment and that which the survivor had expected from the relationship in terms of need gratification. When the deceased is effectively mourned, it is not because gratification is being supplied elsewhere. The survivor has found a way to satisfy his or her needs and desires, in relationship to the beloved lost, internally. Then, with greater ego strength, the mourner develops a different quality and nature of needs and seeks their gratification from sources other than the memory of the deceased. Ideally, a newly transformed position in life allows for, and in fact necessitates, new libidinal attachment in human or nonhuman form.

The biological and physiological bases on which the mourner clings to the notion that the deceased is still extant lies in the initial shock on learning of the death. Shock is the natural response to the immediate disturbance of the survivor's internal equilibrium. The survivor's inner world is disintegrated. He or she is insulted and disorganized. Dazed by the impact of the loss, the signal of danger and emotional pain is initiated, only to be immediately forestalled. From a biological and physiological standpoint, paralleled by psychological parameters, the human organism reacts to the insult, protecting its cohesiveness and continuity by "shutting out" the aggrievement. This is typically a short lived reaction designed to stabilize the integrity of one's personal being, to shore the ego in face of the assault, and to restore one's physical and psychological balance. Whereas other creatures also mourn a significant loss, the human element of the course of bereavement is more sophisticated, if not more agonizing.

In an attachment based on love and intimacy, each partner not only anticipates the confirmed presence of the other, but comes to depend on his or her presence and availability. When a change of any type occurs, the mutually self-enhancing nature of the system is disrupted. If the change is as impinging and devastating as that of death, the survivor's equilibrium begins the long and arduous process of re-stabilization. This is the work of mourning. It involves a great deal of sorrow and suffering, along with an impaired ability to function. The work of mourning is an internal process that attenuates the external reality of loss.[2] Mourning begins and ends within the survivor's inner domain of the mind. He or she will integrate the deceased person into his or her own psychology and sense of self, transform in coordination with this integration, and adapt to the world as it exists without the beloved.

No longer in reality, the lost loved one is sustained within the bereaved's mind where it is not only preserved, but also highly invested with energy and emotion. The relationship continues internally for the survivor. This internal process is accomplished not only as a way of maintaining one's equilibrium in the face of critical onslaught. It additionally serves to transform a real, external loss into an internal, personal, ego loss. Once the profound loss is encapsulated within one's internal world, it is easier to absorb, to scrutinize, to evaluate, and more importantly, to face and deal with. All of the remembrances of the relationship with the lost beloved along with every anticipation of the loved one's existence, is targeted with a tremendous flux of emotional energy. The survivor hypercathects everything that had occurred in loving relationship with the departed. Therewith, the mourner turns away from the outside world and draws inwardly to seemingly safe haven. Internally sustained feelings for the beloved can be dispersed outwardly in optimal doses over a prescribed period of time.

The mourning process of accepting the loss and transforming oneself involves a restructuring of the ego. The bereaved becomes an inherently different person through the course of mourning. This restructuring of the ego differs little from the initial structuring of the child's ego in the formative years. Both the mourner's and the child's ego and sense of the self develop, organize, and reorganize in response to a series of experiences and losses in their external lives. In actuality, the ego does not merely restructure itself; additionally, it continues to grow, build, and sophisticate.

A person mourned had not been loved for just one's own sake. The relationship with the deceased was the means by which the survivor reached his or her ideal self.[3] Loving another is a way of finding and securing a love of oneself. When one is deprived of one's beloved through death, the experience is of not only that loss but also of the loss of the aspect of himself or herself closely identified with the lost beloved. With a depleted sense of self, the ego is overwhelmed and at a heartfelt risk of disintegration. The loss of a love implies subjectively a sense of losing oneself, of dying just like the beloved had died.

A sense of desperation sets in that organizes the mourner's every feeling, thought, and behavior toward the fading but hopeful goal of reuniting with the deceased. Not fully cognizant of the actuality of the loss, a vaguely understood yet profound anxiety ensues. Anxiety, as the normal reaction to a perceived danger, leads to either a fight or flight as a defense.[4] Simultaneous to the danger signal and the reactive anxiety, the ego becomes paralyzed and as it is, unprepared to face the peril. Reactive to the immediate danger, the attending discomfort is that of separation anxiety. Soon thereafter, the pain will be felt.

Pain begins to intersperse with the anxiety and fear as the reality of the loss becomes clearer. Initially, the most readily available defensive and adaptive mechanism is that of weeping. As the shock is attenuated, the response of tearing, whether mildly or voluminously, is the manifestation of sudden feelings of helplessness. When an infant is in temporary absence of the mother, its first response is that of weeping softly and eventually crying vociferously. The infant instinctually employs this mechanism as a way of effectively communicating its distress. So, too, does the mournful adult.[5]

With the sad actualization that the lost loved one is not available and will not return, panic then sets in. Just as the toddler, not yet individuated from the mother, terrors at the recognition of prolonged absence, alarm ripples through the adult. Panic is fear, and fear elicits aggression. Anger is yet another adaptive mechanism employed by the bereaved as a desperate means to demand the immediate return of the lost person.[6] In everyday life, disappointments and unwelcome separations are sometimes remedied by protest and aggressiveness. Angry outbursts can be effective in securing the return of a possession, tangible or intangible, unsolicitedly taken away. But because of the permanence of the deceased's absence, anger and protest, however benevolently activated, nonetheless fail. In time, the bereaved will either surrender to the painful reality or escalate the aggression to the point of destructive behavior to himself or others.

Once the initial shock has concluded and the mechanisms of weeping, crying, anger, and protest have not wielded results, the survivor is challenged with a decision. The survivor is to either accept the loss or defensively and protectively deny it.[7] Decisive action is unconsciously generated by the fear and the pain of the loss and what the loss implies for the bereaved. Additionally, the decision is determined by defense mechanisms geared toward self-preservation. Clearly evident to the bereft, typically, is the need for the acceptance of the loss and next task of the work of mourning. The survivor withdraws emotional energy from the lost person by disconnecting previously cherished desires, hopes, dreams, anticipations, and memories from the deceased. This difficult task comes at a great expense of sorrow and pain. It takes courage to consider a future of uncertainty, a future that embodies oneself, alone, with only one's own resources.

The necessity of change in life is unavoidable. Change is difficult for even the person who has a loved one with whom to pursue the journey of life. In the case of the death of a loved one, a degree of resistance to the change is an option, and typically the one chosen. New ideas, new events, indeed a new life are a painful prospect for the bereaving person. The more distant the world seems with the absence of the loved one, the more one tenaciously clings to the past in fear of the future. Already internally discombobulated, the thought of engaging change is overwhelming to the injured and unequipped ego. The survivor suppresses, and even represses, a host of emotions revolving around the loss. Yet defensively, the most expedient means of ridding the event of the death is to negate, disavow, or diminish the painful fact. Unconsciously, the mourner chooses to continue the relationship with the deceased in fantasy. A mild form of denial serves not only to preserve the loved one, but also constitutes a benevolently adaptive attempt to protect and conserve the ego, lest the survivor disintegrate and psychologically "die" along with the departed.

Negation, disavowal, or outright denial are defense mechanisms thought of as maladaptive, dysfunctional, and abnormal. In the early work of mourning, however, denial in its various forms is considered adaptive. In bereavement, it is not simply the subject who turns from reality because the reality is unbearable and unattenable. The beloved's removal from the subject's world of equilibrium is such an assaultive blow to one's personal integrity that in a very real sense, reality has withdrawn from the subject. Abandoned, the mourner wanders aimlessly in delirium looking helplessly for any degree of connection to a sense of reality, of belongingness, of personal integrity. The ego is stunned, wanting only for the reality that was confiscated from the survivor, and in any form that may yet exist. The injured ego yearns for reattachment, not only specific to the lost loved one, but to life and existence itself. So yearned is an attachment to a world one can be a part of and have a place in. In the acute phase of mourning, this world by necessity becomes an internal world. It is in the survivor's mind that he or she feels some degree of security amidst external disaray, and in which the struggling self can begin the hard work of mourning.

The long course of mourning is a gradual release of bound energy that agonizes the spirit, yet dose by dose frees the mourner of its awesome burden. To experience the immediate entirety of the painful affect of grief would be devastatingly overwhelming. The mourner must carefully diffuse the agony. This process is not only of hard work, but also of all-consuming work. The ego is wholly occupied during the early stages of mourning, providing for the necessarily vigilant circumspection of the mourner's every thought and feeling, as well as the immediate environment which has become so coldly disrupted. All focus is on the mourner's own personhood in the face of uncertainty and fear. The work of mourning is an urgently tedious process of gradually and conscientiously relinquishing each and every emotional tie to the beloved lost.

To attempt to forcefully and unfeelingly expel the beloved from the mourner's existence would be to reject the original relationship shared with the deceased. This indeed would be impossible—much more, a human tragedy. Some bereft individuals find the thought of an eventual disengagement from the deceased so personally intolerable that they break from reality and submit to a psychotic process.

Acceptance of the death of a loved one releases in the mourner a host of both positive and negative emotions that have been harbored for the deceased. Ambivalence is the norm, for every emotion experienced by the survivor is joyfully and painfully reintroduced to him or her over and over again. These very feelings are the ones that must be confronted, worked through, and resolved. Facing the loss of a loved one by death is inherently different than any other experience of loss.

The lifespan of the human is defined and described by a series of losses encountered from birth to death. These losses involve the forfeiture of something dear and valuable to oneself. In order to progress, expand, and confirm one's personhood, one must sadly and painfully let go of certain personal elements. In exchange, the person acquires significantly new aspects of oneself. In an ongoing sequence of losing and gaining a part of the self, humans progressively mature in the promulgation of their own personhood. However, the loss incurred by death is unequivocally cold and harsh, and moreover, permanent. Loss by death does not occupy a transitional point serving as a weigh station for the ushering in of something merely more advanced in a person's development. The permanence of death freezes the heart, demeans the soul, and oppresses the spirit. The mourner loses something that offers no return, no remediation, no substitution, no better-than-before promise for the future. The present is changed and the future is darkly uncertain. In fact, the future seems nil.

It is a necessary yet arduously painful task of the survivor to accept the actuality of a future for oneself. While the memories of the past do not cease, the future includes only oneself in continuity with the memories of the departed one. The normal, healthy course of mourning involves an acceptance and embracement of the past, the present, and the future.

Nature requires the subject to either accept or deny the loss and either progress or stagnate. The mourner's reality sense, along with a healthy respect and love for oneself, shores the weakened ego and challenges the person to mitigate the impingement of the loss. As vague and distant as it may seem to the person in the throes of mourning, hope and will are only transiently diminished. The deceased still holds meaning for the bereaved, and this meaning holds purpose and value for yet the present and the future. The future is what offers the departed the only means of continuation and endurance as embodied and expressed in the life of the survivor.

The future carries hope for the survivor and a vicarious continuity for the remembrance of the deceased, both inviting and encouraging the bereaved to move the mourning process to completion. This is a trial of hardship and endurance. Courage is required to effectively mourn and resultingly transform the self. The courage of personal change places the mourner at the threshold of a strange, new, and intimidating world. Continued defenses may serve to assuage the grief and the sorrow, however maladaptively. Faith and determination, along with a healthy sense of a confirmed and affirmed self, challenge the mourner to engage the struggle on its harsh terms and to overcome. This proceeds for the sake of both oneself and the loving memory of the dear departed.

In time and with effort, successful mourning requires the bereft to transfer the emotional investment in the memory of the lost beloved to the reality of the external world without the departed's presence. Reality sense disallows continued denial of the loss. The intense yearning for the deceased causes the pain and sorrow. The longing and its associated anguish must be tempered by the survivor to the extent that the self-observing and self-preserving ego can tolerate the pain. However cold and unfair the loss is, the key element to uncomplicated mourning is the belief that the survivor's life is simply meant to be, even without the joy and support once provided but now lost. A humbling and genuine appreciation for the departed carries the mourner through the arduous and seemingly merciless encounter with death and misery.

To truly appreciate the departed person, the survivor must fully understand what meaning and value the deceased provided to their relationship. Only by means of this intimate and intricate comprehension can the mourner acknowledge without bias the profound significance that the person of the deceased had, and still holds. Any person who has loved another is consciously aware of what important role the beloved plays in his or her life. While this is a very real and potent awareness, it is yet an only topical understanding of and appreciation for the other person. Below the surface, at a more personal and intimate level of the unconscious lies a more true, symbolically representative significance of the beloved. If the mourner is to effectively let go of the mourned, he or she must to some degree comprehend the deeper, more symbolic meaning of the attachment and the attached person. The symbolic significance of the departed revolves around issues such as dependence and independence, separation and individuation, the projection of an idealized self, and unconditional love, as they formulated prior to the death. The more the mourner comprehends the unconscious symbolism along with the conscious actuality of the departed and their relationship, the more likely that a genuine appreciation and empathy for both the deceased and oneself can be acquired.[8] Resultingly, with a greater empathy and concern for oneself and one's tragic situation, the survivor may muster the personal strength and wisdom to proceed with the painful and sorrowful journey known as the work of mourning.

Ambivalence colors every human relationship. When a loved one dies, the ambivalence does not cease, nor does the relationship. The emotional and personal meaning of the relationship at the point of death becomes more potent and clear to the survivor. All positive and negative feelings toward the departed confront the mourner. Mixed and confused emotions are acutely pronounced and this mitigates the mourner's acceptance of the loss. Conscious or unconscious conflict with the loved one makes it more difficult for the survivor to accept the reality of the loss and let go of the departed with fond feelings. Any disappointment, displeasure, or incomplete amendment leaves the mourner faced with the conflict's fact. It is easier to let go with good feelings than with bad feelings.[9] Good feelings are experienced as complete and offer a sense of fulfillment, while bad feelings are experienced as splitting, spoiling, and depleting. Effective mourning requires the survivor to acknowledge and resolve any ambivalence felt so that letting go of the deceased occurs with acceptance and peace. The attenuation of ambivalence makes it easier for the mourner to experience the sadness necessary to move the mourning process forward in uncomplicated fashion.

The mourner is faced with a two-fold dilemma: He or she must deal with a devastating loss and, as well, any unresolved and unabated ambivalence felt toward the deceased. The survivor adapts to the precariously, indeed dangerously, perceived situation as does the very young child who experiences either separation from, loss of, or unbearable ambivalence toward, the mothering figure. The adaptation is a defensive process experienced internally. Faced with a frightening and overwhelming situation, a crisis indeed, the survivor, like a young child, takes in the pleasurable and gratifying aspects of the person by integrating him or her into the psyche. Just as the child utilizes the internalized mother image to allay the anxiety incurred by the critical situation of absence from the much needed and desired mother, so, too, does the mourner draw from the deceased's internal presence to sooth and contain himself or herself in the face of crises and distress. Sustained internally, the survivor can scrutinize, manage, and utilize the internal representation of the deceased as a means of allaying the flood of sorrow, grief, and emotional pain. The internalization process encourages the healthy illusion of a continued relationship with the departed.

As noted in earlier chapters, the human organism is constitutionally geared toward achieving emancipation, individuation, and autonomy. As nature has it, the nascent ego of the child internalizes the needed aspects of significant persons to carry with him and to utilize them internally as building blocks for his own ego and self-structure. The survivor of death is similarly propelled to sustain one's ego integrity, face the loss with strength, and promote self-sufficiency. Another's death can encourage personal reflection and promote an eerie feeling of impending doom. For this reason, defensive maneuvering against the anguish becomes both a purpose and a goal in and of itself. The loss of a loved one is perceived not only as an unsolicited deprivation of the spirit of the survivor but as a direct threat to one's very being.

In desperation and fear, the mourner is naturally driven to find some means of mastering the loss. This urgency creates an internal struggle as one part of the ego attempts to confront the crisis while the another wishes to escape its clutches. As previously noted, the struggle is ameliorated by the willingness and propensity to honor both wishes by accepting the loss piecemeal in gradually dosed confrontation with the loss. The survivor yearns for and seeks the departed only to repeatedly find him or her gone. Each failed attempt to recapture his or her presence incrementally accentuates the person's unavailability and the resulting grief. The internalization process the survivor undergoes compensates for the small but steady depletion of the ego. This process attenuates the anguish of the loss by repeatedly yearning for the lost loved one and having to acknowledge his or her absence. As mentioned, it is the intense longing for the much desired person that creates the emotional turmoil.[10]

The work of mourning is, for protective and adaptive reasons, an internal experience. The overwhelming emotions felt are modulated by transforming an external loss into an internal loss. Internally, the mourner acquires the ability to scrutinize the situation more closely and emotionally control his or her response to the crisis. All feelings are directed toward the internalized image of the deceased. The relationship continues, though on a different plane. Ultimately, it is the mourner's task to loosen the exclusive tie to the departed in favor of forming new attachments to new persons of the external world. This, too, is painfully trying. The beleaguered ego protects itself by preserving the loving bond to the departed by carrying the relationship internally and gradually relinquishing it in small doses as determined bearable. The work of mourning is psychologically easier to accomplish if it is pursued internally rather than externally with real life events. It is easier for the mourner to calculatingly relinquish an attachment to an internalized representation than it is to an existing person of external reality.

An internally sustained relationship is highly personalized. The mourner replays every previous emotional encounter with the lost loved one. As a way of protecting oneself, as well as the integrity of the departed, the mourning ego finds it easier to focus on the loving, positive feelings towards the deceased and diminish the negative. There is a natural tendency to honor and cherish the goodness of the departed and to pardon any perceived malignancies. Resultingly, the relationship with the dear departed may become posthumously more intimate and focused, and an identification with the deceased becomes sharper and clearer. This identification, more sophisticated than that of a child seeking satisfaction of needs, is based solely in honor of the lost loved one. The mourner comes to terms with the admiring and respecting components of his or her own ego, advancing the quality of the identification and offering greater service to the mourner's ego. The mourner's personality strengthens and expands in heightened appreciation for the departed and for having had the experience of intimate attachment.

At the completion of the mourning process, the survivor has gone through a change in self-structure that permits and encourages the strengthened ego to carry on in a life absent the deceased. In time, the survivor becomes capable of engaging a new love while healthily sustaining existing loves. Having healthily identified with the deceased, the mourner becomes to a degree like the deceased. In spirit, the mourner once again captures the lost person. At this phase of the mourning process, separation from the deceased is experienced as less of a deprivation and more of a liberation from the sorrow and the grief. Mastery of the loss makes the ego stronger and the person self-reliant in spite of the loved one's absence. In time, mourning gives way to strength, personal courage, and emancipation.

Internalization of the lost loved one serves initially to defensively protect the mourner from the pain. Identification with the internalized deceased serves to compensate for the incurred loss. Identifying with the cherished aspects of the departed allows for a closer, healthier, less ambivalently charged relationship that the mourner internally sustains with the lost beloved. But through the work of mourning, internalization ceases to be a mere defense against the pain of loss. It transforms into a desired and reparative objective, an end in and of itself holding promise not of permitting the mourner to hold on to the dear departed, but encouraging the mourner to seek emancipation from the deceased and punctuate one's own individuality as it includes, but not relegated to, the lost beloved. As a result of the liberation, the deceased is viewed more realistically than perhaps ever before. The departed beloved is seen not so much as a lost object of loving companionship, but as a unique person with distinct ideals, goals, and dreams, experienced separately from the mourner.

It is not only the mourned who is perceived in a different and more valued light. The mourner also transforms in face of the painful crisis of loss by death. As mentioned earlier, as insultive and disruptive as the loss indeed is, the survivor experiences a healthy reconstruction of his or her own personality. Like an adolescent who relinquishes childhood innocence and security when severing ties to his parents, the mourner finds himself enriched, along with a self-perceived increase in strength, wisdom, and courage. The reason for this heightened sense of personal awareness and reorganization is because the mourner comes to embody the departed and carry him or her within.[11,12] The deceased is never truly lost. The person lost becomes a part of the person survived. A loving attachment to the departed is, in effect, reconstructed and continued anew.

The internalized loved one not only strengthens the mourner's ego, but contributes to an ego-ideal toward which the mourner strives. In progressive movement toward regained normalcy, the survivor no longer desires to regressively merge with the deceased, but is guided by new ideals that are both realistic and adaptive. These ideals are founded on the cherished and admired aspects of the departed's personality that are now embodied and expressed by the mourner.

The person of the mourner perpetuates the person of the mourned. The mourner, in effect, assumes the pleasurable and satisfying activities that the loved one had engaged. The mourner may pursue with avid interest activities that were regularly enjoyed by the deceased. Upon death, the mourner may also honor any of the departed's wishes of pursuing particular goals or experiencing certain events. Examples have been noted of women who, upon their husband's death, have continued to own and manage their husband's business. This is done, at least partially, in attempt to carry on the husband's legacy, capture his dreams, and vicariously prove his commitment and efficacy. His dreams may become her drive. The survivor is therewith able to continue to gratify the lost loved one. Moreover, identification paradoxically sharpens the mourner's sense of differentiation from the deceased, which in turn, offers an easing of the pain and the hardship of having to let go.

The function of locating one's ego-ideal in specific activities of the deceased allows the mourner to constructively discharge emotional energy that otherwise remains, as in the early stages of mourning, desperately and hopelessly bottled. Loving energy for the departed in reality, upon death, has no immediate target for discharge. Perhaps it is the build up of energy forcefully contained that contributes to the extreme pain and anguish. Identifications with the deceased encourage a gradual discharge of emotions while simultaneously expanding and enriching the mourner's ego. This is a safe and tenable means by which the survivor can accomplish the hard work of mourning and accept the reality of the beloved's departure and irretrievability.

In silent repose, the pained mourner collects and constitutes himself or herself in preparation of once again confronting and greeting the external world on its own terms. These terms seem to harden the person's view of the world with the permanent absence of the departed. But, daily activities are able to be met and the unenviable mourner slowly releases ties to the deceased. Each activity in which the mourner participates without the presence of the deceased serves as a painful reminder of the beloved's departure. Memories are bitter-sweet and love is lamented. The survivor engages these activities alone, yet the ego is increasingly strengthened and encouraged. In time, the mourner becomes less consumed by the memories that such activities evoke. Resultingly, there is a gradual emotional detachment from the departed, freeing the ego to libidinally invest in other persons.

As previously mentioned, the mourner internalizes and identifies with precious aspects of the deceased. With each experience in the external world that retrieves the painful, yet good, memories of the departed, there is a paralleled detachment from the internalized mourned. The ego becomes increasingly fortified and assured as it utilizes the internalization process to shore the self. Subsequent identifications with the deceased become part of the mourner's personality and allow him to de-intensify the memories by becoming "at one" with the lost loved one. There is then a steady diminishing of the sorrow, grief, and sadness as the mourner proceeds with life.

Repeated confirmation of the departed's unavailability couples with the recognition that the desire for the beloved's return is a futile wish. In the case of the loss of a spouse, it becomes increasingly fathomable to the mourner to possess a desire for a new partner and to invest oneself emotionally in a new relationship. This phenomenon is made possible by the survivor's eventual ability and propensity to perceive the deceased less so in terms of the latter's actual person. In essence, the mourner perceives, acknowledges, and most importantly, appreciates the departed more so for what he or she represents symbolically. Typically, the symbolic meaning includes the precious elements that provide for friendship, companionship, and intimation. Once the mourner is able and willing to recognize, understand, and accept the symbolic significance of the deceased, it becomes even easier to envision another person filling a similar role. This leads to personal strength, growth, and the courage to move on with the departed embodied, carried, and lived honorably by the survivor.

Refreshed and newly prepared for the pursuit of new attachments in a world brightened with hope and opportunity, the long burdened mourner pursues life with creative vigor. The personality organization of the mourner, now embodying and living that which was cherished in the departed beloved, is transformed and reorganized into a person stronger, wiser, and more courageous than ever.

Chapter Eleven

Primary Love in Summary

The person of one's being, the very essence of one's selfhood, is instituted wholly and directly from the primordial experience of envelopment with the first object of love—the motherly mother. Blissful fusion, indeed incorporation, with the essential attachment figure comprises the total life of the newborn infant, as well as significantly of any adult who forever wishfully yearns for its reoccurrence. What one experiences in the prime of life is an existence in approximation of perfection, of unison, of freedom from distress. Unquestionably, the symbiosis of mother and her progeny is based solidly on their biologically determined attachment. Each party is by nature's way physiologically and biochemical set to be in tune to one another's needs and inherent tendencies, expressed largely by bodily contact and communicative interaction. Physiologically predetermined, the innately dictated relationship between the infant and its urgently needed mother serves the basis for the formation of an undisputed and unequivocally psychological relationship. The emotionality of the attachment from the very earliest is founded on the infant's archaically and subjectively felt pleasure and displeasure. Though the baby is conceptually unaware of separation and distinction between itself and the ministering mother, there is nonetheless an intricate and exquisite emotional connection between them. Each precisely elicits affectivity from the other, speaking clearly to the truth of their bond. Primary love is present at birth.

Relationship tendencies and potentials are cast at birth with both the mother and the father. The specific features of these relationships are formulated by the newborn on how mother and father are felt to exist. Shortly after birth, the baby senses and feels a difference between what it experiences in relatedness to mother and in relatedness to father. The infant elicits and responds to mother's presence and activity in a variety of ways and with differing interactions and need states. Father is perhaps more vague, nondescript, and difficult to fathom in the fledgling child's yet incapacity to conceptualize its social and physical environment. Yet, father's presence is real and the experiences with him are potent.

In emotional connection with both the mother and father, the infant vests its loved objects with pleasure and goodness. Mother, particularly, becomes the "good," gratifying object, and from this human encounter, the infant's ego begins to formulate. Moreover, the infantile self develops the capacity to love and be loved, an experience of contentedness and pleasure that sets the foundation for a sense of security and happiness. In a yet primitive and fundamental way, the infant is primed for feeling gratitude for its mother and her generous love and intimation. And the pliable self is readied to return mother's offerings in the form of its own archaic, yet very certain, expression of love.

From the highly emotionally charged encounters develop a sense of safety and security, and therewith a sense of confidence and trust. Love is firmly established and integrated with not only a mental representation of the good, pleasurable mother, but equally important, a consistent mental image of a good, giving and receiving self. This personal experience is solidified by the repeated encounters of intimating with the mother in mutual cooing, gaze, and touch. The baby is fed, the baby is satiated, and the baby quiesces into slumber. This is the all-goodness, the oceanic feeling of oneness, the bliss and ecstasy of primary love.

These repeated encounters and their increasing enforcement of confidence and trust in one's experience with the mother, allow the infant to develop the basic building blocks with which it constructs all subsequent relationships, including with the exciting, other-than-mother figure of the father. The infant ego strengthens and the baby acquires the beginnings of self-concept and esteem.

Through infancy, accumulated memory traces of pleasure at the hands of the gratifying mother become loosely, yet increasingly sufficiently, connected to the external person of the mother. Pleasurable memory traces build and formulate a memory structure that comes to represent the good, pleasurable mother. The percept of mother is thusly based on actual experiences with her. By means of repeated good experiences with mother and a paralleled reinforcement of a sensed goodness of the yet primitive self in attachment to her, the infant solidifies its image of the available mother. She is perceived, however vaguely yet importantly, as a source who exists, who is present, and who is giving. The totality of the mother's existence revolves around and encompasses the infant's overall experience of being mothered—of being mothered by a body of flesh and comfort.

With a crystallizing awareness of the mother's presence and availability, the infant-child acquires a functional sense of control of its self-system of input and output, of receiving and giving in mutual interaction with the mothering figure. Intentionality forms as the infant directs its behavior with stimuli of its choice based on the child's current needs and desires. The infant fixes its gaze onto the mother's inviting face. It kicks and grasps for mother's bodily contact. Cooing and smiling, the baby cues to its mother that it is attracted to her and wants her. Likewise, the infant uses social cueing from the mother to prolong and enjoy its attentive state. Intentionality also takes the form of shutting out mother when its needs and wishes bid for quiet and private time and space. And a child of just several weeks shows signs of wish for a return to mother's loving presence. With gratitude, the infant wishes to do something for her. Baby wishes to hold and cuddle its mother as she holds and cuddles her deserving progeny. Reaching for and touching mother's mouth may be an indication of wishing to orally gratify her just as the infant is orally gratified at the mother's breast or bottle. This is love at its very source.

In fact, the child of infancy has marked influence on the psychology and sociality of the mother. The mutuality of the mother-infant experience is highlighted by the interactional impact each has on the other. It has been noted how the mother ushers in the burgeoning self of her offspring through her loving ministrations. It is this same transactional process that beckons and reinforces the very maternal aspects of a woman that have hitherto been lying dormant. Maternal instinct is biologically predetermined, the course of which is nonetheless inspired by the unique being of her beloved child.

It is universal to mothering for women to intuitively and graciously emulate and mimic their young infants. Mother mirrors her baby's behaviors. When her baby makes certain, especially new, facial expressions reflective of its mood and state of mind, mother imitates those expressions in the gesture of love, acceptance, and encouragement. The infant begins to acquire confidence in itself to have influence with its social world, a type of authority that it yet does not have with the physical objects of its environment. Gratefully, the infant recognizes that it does in fact have an influence on mother's behavior. This is rewarding and self-promoting for the baby, as well as exciting to the mother who elates at the actualization of her own maternal, instinctual proclivities. Mother, too, activates her personhood in parallel to the developing self of her loved one.

With self-determination and effort, the infant-child achieves its social aims. The infant projects its own experience into the mothering figure who, in mirroring the projection, allows her baby to reinternalize and assimilate the experience, thereby providing the rudiments of self-image. As the infant feels securely contained in mother's loving presence, it projects its sense of well-being and social effectiveness into the facilitating mother who, in her self-acclaimed efficiency in good mothering, joyfully mirrors her and her baby's pleasure and contentment in return to her progeny. Baby absorbs its own reflection embellished and reinforced by mother's involvement, assuring for itself not only a fundamental sense of being, but a being both capable and worthy of eliciting and claiming mother's love and approval. Maternal mirroring in this way fosters the infant's gradual acquisition of selfhood and differentiation. In turn, the mother feels herself to be a necessarily vital component of the self-system of her burgeoning child. Likewise, the infant feels itself to be an integral part of mother's personal experience. The circularity of this growth enhancing matrix provides for and promotes love, intimacy, and attachment. And not lastly, it fosters hope and inspiration for both mother as a parent and child as a maturing person.

Maternal mirroring promotes the infant's sense of achievement and competence in having influence on its environment. This encourages the gradual process of separation and differentiation from the mothering person. Individuation and identity are initiated. The infant's sense of separateness and individuality is ushered in by the very space between itself and the much needed and aspired mother. During mother's temporary and necessary absences in the course of her ministering services, the world of the infant is experienced within the space between the self and the mother. This space becomes the outer world as it exists in the realm of the other-than-me-and-mother domain. As mother intuitively permits her baby's time of solitude and privacy, she introduces her loved one to the world of reality as she knows it, and as the child will come to know it. She also facilitates her baby's beginning sense of autonomy in this new world. Mother relinquishes the symbiosis in part to allow her child to become optimally independent in its environment. Her baby acquires the ability to initiate, respond to, and modulate its own experiences with physical as well as social objects.

As infancy proceeds and toddlerhood approaches, the baby begins to create more expansively the space between itself and mother by climbing down from her and crawling away. Distancing oneself from the mother of attachment, the ensuing toddler explores the new world and revels in the experience of self-initiation, autonomy, and competence. The meaning of attachment assumes a new quality for both child and mother. With the discovery of a world beyond the mother-and-me unit, the infant confronts toddlerhood with new social and physical encounters. These encounters in bodily activity with toys and games, along with social activity with outside others like father and older siblings, repeatedly and pointedly reveal to the young child that he and his mother are not alone in this world and do not comprise life's entirety. Moreover, what is understood by the toddler is that there exists certain aspects of mother that have nothing to do with him, and likewise that there are elements of himself and his own experience that do not include mother. Differentiation between the self and the life-preserving, enveloping mother of symbiosis is heralded. This constitutes a milestone in psychosocial development.

Self-other differentiation is conceptually accomplished only gradually over the course of the toddler years of approximately ten to thirty-six months as the child's cognitive, language, affective, and bodily capacities strengthen and flourish. The child is elated with his or her toddler activities and enticed by his or her personal mastery. Yet emotionally the child is in a quandary. Losing the graciously granted attention and protection of mother's enveloping arms and incorporating goodness is nature's harsh price for maturation. Mother, too, faces the unenviable task of relinquishing the bliss and ecstasy of being in meld with the very product of her being. Yet, nature has its course, and by its dictates, both toddler and mother rise to the challenge and the sadness of separation and individuation by elevating the nature and quality of their everlasting attachment.

On a new psychological and social, no less than physical, plane, mother and child not only do not lose or diminish the power of their mutual love. Their love, in fact, sophisticates and expands. Love means so much more than suckling at the generous breast, and so much more than gazing into one another's eyes and seeing the wonderment of their united souls. Love now acknowledges and appreciates the miracle of autonomy, of growth, the unfolding of a personal being. And this is not only in reference to the toddler child. Any mother attests, with tears of joy, how she so intricately and delicately grows herself with every step of her loving progeny's development. Far from relinquishing the bond of love, their mutual affinity captures the present and promises a future with intimate experiences that serve only to preserve, testify to, and reverently honor the love of primacy.

It is expressedly out of the love that the mother and her toddler hold for one another that separation and individuation proceed effectively. The child's initiative in increasingly selecting maternal behaviors to which to respond helps to formulate himself as a budding person of his own personal needs and impulses. The love of toddlerhood with its inherent separation and individuation owes its higher order of definition to the very differentiation between the selves of the toddler and his mother. Love certainly means more to the toddler aged child as he looks to his gratifying mother as an independent source of activity. Appreciation and gratitude for mother's efforts become more focused and clarified. This is why the toddler acquires such joy and inspiration as he makes his first autonomous moves away from mother. With every step he takes toward liberation, he makes a subsequent move back to her. In the process, he experiences the pleasure and assurance of rediscovering the good mother. With each rediscovery, the increasingly autonomous toddler obtains a new and more matured view of mother in all her support and availability. Similarly, every venture into the other-than-me and other-than-mother world provides him with a new and more realistic view of what the external world is all about.

It is precisely this expanding perspective of himself, his mother, and the world of reality that he brings back to mother's waiting arms. He delights in showing her his independent acquisitions and his expanding selfhood. He wishes to share his creation of liberation with the favoring and encouraging mother of goodness, who, by means of her loving approval and stability, remains the center of life and the hub of his wheel of exploration. Mother's loving service is her progeny's home base and provides him with initiative and inspiration. The definitive core of love as it is demonstrated between the emancipating and differentiating toddler and his permissible and encouraging mother assumes a significantly active measure. No longer in passive meld with the mother of symbiosis, the adventurous child now more actively claims his self-experiences and equally actively expresses his love and gratitude for mother's acceptance and continuity.

By the end of toddlerhood, love is experienced by two autonomous persons rather than by two constituent elements of a single unit. The child of three years feels powerful and competent in this new paradigm of intimate relationship with his or her mother. Yet, there is a price to pay for maturity and ego advancement. The subjective experience of primary attachment transforms into an objective self-perception and awareness. As the child acknowledges his differentiation and distinctiveness as a human being, he also acknowledges, and painfully so, his capacity and occasion to feel alone. His once all-encompassing tie to mother is no longer an actuality. Frightened and pained at times in response to this realization, the child privately longs for his mother and the return to absolute unison. The state of longing coalesces with a sharpened sense of separateness as the two experiences intensify more emotionally than intellectually and conceptually. In nature's way, nonetheless, it is this very longing for mother's presence that in actuality strengthens, enhances, and matures the loving attachment between the uncertain child and his challenged mother. Mother's ministrations in service to the needs of her child are now outweighed in importance to the child by her mere constancy, her willful desire to be available to her loved one, now recognized by both parties as an individuated person. This gives new significance and meaning to love. Now that love cannot be taken for granted by the child, its presence and acknowledgement is far more appreciated.

To preserve and enhance the love the young child feels between the persons of himself and his mother, he forms an identification with her. The young child internalizes his mother's goodness in all of its aspects and formulates a preciously held identification with this internalization. This crystallizes his sense of comfort in knowing of her emotional availability even as, and especially when, mother is increasingly absent. An integral part of his maternal identification is the child's wish to be more like her, especially within the realm of her adult characteristics. The child lovingly admires mother's strength, wisdom, and autonomy, and strives to emulate these characteristics. Control of the bodily functions, including bowel and bladder effectiveness, is all- important to the child of three years. Social engagement of other children and grownups affords the child the opportunity to relate to people with the ease and assurance he feels with his mother. Above all, in every sense, the loving and lovable child wishes to capture mother's approval and receive her commendation. Identity burgeons with these accomplishments and the child's increasingly cohesive sense of personhood is contingent on such like-mother acquisitions.

Becoming like mother substitutes, then, for being at one with her. Carrying mother's loving and generative functions within oneself, the young child is empowered to take occupancy and ownership of his or her life and experience it to the fullest. The child recognizes mother as an independent source of her own desire and activity, and in parallel acknowledges himself as his own center of initiative. In separation from the mother, the natural losses incurred become increasingly tolerable to the aspiring child. His sense of oneness with the mother and her goodness abates in favor of a sense of oneness with the goodness and the person of himself. Passivity at the hands of mother's loving ministrations evolves into the young child's self-inaugurated activity. With mother's gentle yet certain urgence, her child learns to engage the social and physical world and performs by his own merit. The child activates his life as mother approvingly applauds and prides herself with both his and her accomplishment.

Identification with the mother and her goodliness becomes increasingly the internal mechanism by which the child gauges the expanding world and confronts it by means of his own initiative. The internalized mother, so endearingly identified with, is carried within as an ego-supportive mainstay. As both the female and male child achieves individuation at the close of toddlerhood and traverses the path of the oedipal situation, another psychosocial milestone is reached. The child liberates, free to face life with autonomy and self-sufficiency. Yet, there remains so carefully processed and so intuitively understood, a continued dialogue, both verbal and nonverbal, between the mother and her emancipating child. The loving partners retain elements of periodic and transient experiences of oneness. Paradoxically, each party feels a simultaneous sense of merger and separateness. This experience is particularly supportive to the oedipal aged child of three to five or six years because it significantly colors the ongoing love with mother with a special quality and brilliance. Love, now, is contingent in its intensity and provision on two distinct and separate persons, mother and child, who almost impercep-tively yet choreographically move toward and into one another engagingly, only to disengage one another with the beat of each partner's personal and interpersonal needs. Love will never again be identified by fusion and mutual encapsulation. However, never to die will be the temporary and occasional regressions in subjective experience to the cherished togetherness of primary love. Mother and child will never decline an opportunity for warm embrace and shared activity, and for mutual succorance and affirmation.

The expanding social world of the oedipal child necessitates the timely dis-engagement of mother and child. Father's role, having had great significance on the infant's and toddler's development, now assumes a uniquely different function. The nature of the relationship between the father and his daughter or son changes precisely because the nature of the girl's or boy's relationship to their mother alters. As the mother lets go of her child of either gender, the father concurrently "takes in" his child providing a new type of social engagement. The good father offers the oedipal child the freedom and means by which to disengage mother. However, the father's new function proceeds with some ill-ease, especially for the male child. Envy and rivalry set in.

The oedipal boy is perceived by mother as the gender opposite, destined definitively for emancipation. She acknowledges that her son is to secure firm ego boundaries by means of immersing himself in his newfound indi-viduation. Mother's beloved progeny takes his first step toward manhood to become someday like his father. The father, in all his goodliness, is nonetheless intimidated to some degree by his son's newly acquired vigor and assertiveness. Awakened within every father are unresolved oedipal is-sues from his own childhood that revolve around aggression, potency, and the wish to forcefully secure the strength of manhood so occupied by his own oedipal father. Moreover, father lingers in the yet unresolved guilt that this normal oedipal wish instills so firmly in the psyche and is carried into adulthood. Unconsciously, the father, out of love for his oedipal aged son, struggles to keep his unresolved anxiety, fear, and guilt in check so as not to aggressively overburden or afflict his beloved child. He wishes only for his son to be secure with his newfound liberation and positioning in the world, and to happily promulgate the burgeoning person that he is, in all the child's unfolding masculinity.

From generation to generation there is an uneasy emotional transmission of oedipal struggle with the man's own, and his son's budding, manliness. The oedipal boy senses this emotional struggle, experiences it, and significantly labors with it. Indeed, the so-called rivalry between father and son is born principally from this universal phenomenon. Father is not jealous of and rivalrous with his male offspring. He is simply intimidated by his own anxieties which are internalized and vicariously experienced by the boy and become the impetus for the boy's guilt in response to his own aggressiveness. This experience is not a sign of psychological pathology. Quite the contrary, it is a clear indication of the love, the concern, and the delicate care that the good father so endearingly assumes in the role of fatherhood. Father contains his own ambivalence toward masculinity and manhood, and more specifically toward individuation, so as to likewise help contain his beloved son in the latter's nascence and naiveté concerning the same venture into maleness. The father's and the son's tasks are born from a mutual experience and become a shared undertaking. So as it is, a joint resolution is in order. Yet, a resolution is never completed. The child internalizes father's empathic concern, carries it to his own fathering experience, and utilizes it in loving identification with the father in securing comfort for his own oedipal aged son. Though the oedipal conflict is never completely resolved, under the auspices of love, it is attenuated in a compromise formation.

The oedipal aged girl is in a unique situation of her own. Her relationship to father is one of excitement, joy, and exhilaration. Father is the wonderful target of the little girl's affection. While the girl may well be somewhat cautious and uncertain of father's overt strength and potency in regard to the way he fascinates and enravishes her, she nonetheless pursues him with minimal reservation. This is in part due to the fact that father represents to the female child the afforded opportunity to disengage from the mother of primary attachment. This experience is fraught with ambivalence for both the oedipal girl and her mother.

The mother feels in continuity with her daughter because of a feminine gender identification. It is likely that mother will experience her daughter as more of an extension of herself and resultingly decline to let go of her as readily as she does her son. The primacy of the mother-daughter relationship prolongs. In the truest sense, separation completes itself at a later age for the female child. This phenomenon explains the seemingly intractable love-hate ambivalence to which females attest in the mother-daughter attachment. The father bodes well in this encounter in his service as an alternate attachment figure with whom intimacy is of a different nature. The girl's identity as a female is defined greatly by her acknowledgement that her father sees her femininity in a differing, yet equally precious, light than he views his wife's femininity. This helps strengthen and support the oedipal girl's continuing individuation and personality formation. As the girl recognizes and accepts her father's attachment to mother and her inability to claim him exclusively, she comes to appreciate him for his exciting and inviting other-than-mother aspects. She also comes to lovingly appreciate mother for her presence and availability as the ideal model by which to formulate her identity as a female, with all her mother's inherent goodliness.

With the advent of adolescence, the girl particularly experiences ambivalence toward her mother with whom she has so lovingly identified, yet to whom she is often overly attached with fluid boundaries. Toddler and oedipal issues concerning ego boundaries and differentiation, not completely resolved, are replayed in adolescence. This experience has equal psychological impact on the teen girl and her mother. Additionally, the healthy identification of the girl with her mother and the latter's gracious allowance for this identification, holds great potential for pulling both mother and daughter through the mutually held ambivalence and guiding them through the tumultuous adolescent task of recapitulating the separation and individuation of toddlerhood and finalizing its accomplishment. If all goes well, the emergence from primary love culminates in the acquisition of a mature relationship based on a mutual identification of an adult with a soon-to-be adult, a woman with a soon-to-be woman.

Not only are the experiences of love during toddlerhood and Oedipus replayed with their inherent tasks and struggles, they are also intensified and augmented during adolescence. Adolescent love is replete with losses and gains, tragedies and joys, and humility and fulfillment. This is nature's way, and the tenuous process of teenage love is designed to promote the successful completion of transition from the sensual and intimate innocence of childhood to the sexual and personal maturity of adulthood. It is, in fact, the very transient nature of teen relationships of intimacy and the repeated encounters of love gained and love lost that progressively lead the adolescent girl and boy to the stabilization of personal and sexual identity. Each love relationship and its relinquishment delivers the teen step by step from the throes of childhood parental ties to the acquisition of the mature love, intimacy, and attachment of adulthood.

This maturational process comes with significant emotional and social hardship for the aspiring teenager. Not only must the teen relinquish his first love objects, he also lets go of the parental ideals with which he has identified. Venturing into the extra-familial world of contemporaries, the adolescent creates ideals, values, and goals of his own that will guide him into the adult world as a person in his own right. As he withdraws investment in his parents, his energy flows inwardly to the self. The teenager's investment in the self means to some degree a withdrawal from the outside world of reality. This is a regression to the early childhood experience of narcissism wherein the child feels a sense of omnipotence and self-sustained security. Narcissistic withdrawal is the norm during early adolescence. It serves as an adaptive mechanism lending to the avoidance of being left alone in the teen world of reality unprotected, without the security of infantile ties to the parents, and with a yet underdeveloped ego strength with which to engage this expanding world.

Adolescence is replete with narcissistic injury. Teenagers fall in their social and emotional encounters, and sometimes simply picking oneself up from the fall and carrying on is insufficient. Regression, withdrawal, and isolation offer the beleaguered teen the opportunity to safely contain and observe oneself, reflect on oneself, and recapture a personal sense of valuation and esteem. This is accomplished to a great extent without external support, though with yet significant inner support of the internally sustained parents. Even though the adolescent's ego-ideal is transforming into one determined by his or her unique personality and his or her own life experiences in the social and physical world, these new ideals are based solidly on the identifications the teen has formed during childhood with the good mother and father, as well as significant others. In this light, the parents remain internally suspended in the teenager's psyche, guiding him or her with much needed illumination along the path of adolescent uncertainty.

Adolescent withdrawal affords the periodically injured youth a home base to which to return for the consolidation of self-structure and an emotional refueling with which to venture once again into the adolescent social world. The search for new love objects continues and when a new loved one is found, the ego is shored and ready to invest libidinal energy in the new, special person. It is imperative that the adolescent concurrently give up primary loved ones as he ventures forth in search of new, contemporary ones. Of equal importance, the parents are tasked with enduring their teenager's need to withdraw from them, and at times even repudiate them. The teen's false sense of omnipotence wears heavily on the parents and it is incumbent on their effective parenting to sustain the psychological onslaught, to avoid their own social devaluation, and to accept individual limitations as persons not only of adulthood but also of their own adolescent experiences past. The loving mother and father effortly avoid projecting their self-limitations and failures into their offspring. They repress or otherwise contain the sadness of lost aspirations and unfulfilled dreams. The parents' earlier formed identifications with their parents of childhood and unresolved conflicts surface intensely as their children reach the pubertal teen years. Unless assuaged, fertile ground exists for the resurgence of old struggles. This transgenerational phenomenon does, however, also provide opportunity for the parents to "work through" and resolve past conflicts and failures in the context of their current relationships with their adolescent children. And this is accomplished to the extent that parents acknowledge their child's differentiation and individuation, and provide a healthy and stable model for their children's identification with them.

A healthy identification with the parents is noted by the child's wish to be like them. Indeed, during adolescence, in devaluation of his parents' ideals, aspirations, and accomplishments, the teen wishes to pronounce his own virtues and capabilities and forge his own identity. Yet, from the beginning the child's wish is to become like the parents. Old identifications do not die. They may modify with life's experiences through the lifespan; however, the foundation of a parental identification remains forever solid and activated. This is clearly exemplified by the child's desire, heightened during late adolescence and shared adulthood with the parents, to repay mother and father for their gracious offerings of love, empathy, protection, support, and affirmation. This is a very personal goal of the adolescent as he relinquishes his childhood and comprehends the vital function the parents have so diligently assumed. As the teen thinks about adulthood, his heartfelt aspiration is to soon be the parent of goodness that has so distinguished his own parents. The teenager wishes to emulate the actuality of his parents, therewith humbly acknowledging his own vulnerability and dependence of childhood and genuinely appreciating the fact that his mother and father assume their parental responsibilities so carefully. This is gratitude and love, the impetus and groundwork from which the teen eventually secures the mature love, intimacy, and attachment with another adult.

For both the adolescent and the parents, early childhood conflicts are never completely resolved or abated. They do, however, become less encompassing and consuming. Internal conflicts and personal dissatisfactions toward the end of adolescence are more acknowledged and attenable. They become integrated into who the adolescent is, and therewith serve as the motivator and generator of directed life goals and tasks. Each time the teen experiences a conflict and successfully resolves it, the result is a building of ego strength and a rising of personal esteem. He feels accomplished in not only having solved a dilemma and being relieved of its attending anxiety, but also in having had the introspective capacity to recognize his distress and its source. This is maturity.

Life's aspirations and activities represent the adolescent's expressed wish to meet his ego-ideal, to overcome his weaknesses and shortcomings, and to feel good about himself in the process. By the close of adolescence, the youth acquires a moral sense that inherently personifies his dignity and self-valuation. He neither follows the dictates of parental constriction nor permits his instinctual desires for unqualified gratification to guide his morality and ethical sense. Having relied as a child on parental direction and influence, the teenager on the brink of adulthood now relies on his own personhood as it has been constructed by the ongoing relationship between he and his parents since its inception. The young woman and man for the remainder of life display a pattern of decision making, sacrifices, and self-demands that meet, confirm, and preserve the personal sense of dignity so uniquely and preciously acquired.

The reward is reaped. At the close of adolescence, the young adult constructs for himself or herself under the modeling and encouraging auspices of the good mother and father, a new and emotionally heightened relationship with his or her procreators. They are now adult to adult. Yet, the love is still there, the intimation persists, and the attachment is forever secured. Now the relationship is maturationally advanced and sophisticated. By this means, the parents lovingly hold on to their child otherwise lost. They pride themselves with the accomplishment of having witnessed their progeny successfully grow up to become an adult—their adult child. The adult child is gratefully surprised to seemingly suddenly discover himself to be an adult, positioned integrally in the adult world. Identification is the cornerstone of this phenomenal acquisition as adult child and parents come to share common interests, values, and ideals along with appreciating differences in the same realms. It is a long and precarious process of separation and individuation for both the child and the parents from birth to the threshold of adulthood. And parents take loving pride in the pride their adult child feels for himself.

An important task is at hand. At the reach of adulthood the young woman or man has secured for herself or himself a consistent, coherent, and solid identity. The young adult knows who she or he is as a person among other persons and one of gender specificity. A strong biopsychosocial push expresses itself in fervent wish to promulgate one's gender identity, one's sexual desire and proclivity, and one's personhood as a viable adult. The young adult looks for her or his position in the adult world. Education, career, friendships, and an adult-to-adult relationship with each parent serve to add dimension and clarity to the young adult's expressed selfhood. These adult activities, manifestly mature as they indeed are, are pronouncements of one's ego advancement and progressive movement toward becoming the ultimate person whom one is to be. Ego development is of course the norm, yet forward movement as it engenders accomplishment and pride leaves the youthful adult with a vague, yet very real and impinging sense of loss and emptiness. What is missing is essentially one's past, a bygone existence identified by and enjoyed with the innocence and security of childhood. More specifically, the young adult longs for the lost bliss and harmony of the primal experience of being in loving oneness with the providing mother. As one joyfully experiences the present and pursues the future, one also sorrowfully memorializes the past. All previous encounters of both pleasure and hardship recognizably culminate in the very person of uniqueness that one so assuredly is. In honor of oneself, one only reluctantly and painfully—indeed psychopathologically, desires and chooses to disavow the past, negate one's personal experiences, and minimize one's rite of passage into the present and that which the present so blessedly holds for the future. To partake in fond memory of one's personal development is to genuinely appreciate one's presence, one's existence, one's contribution to and purpose for the future.

To the truth of the human's initial and most meaningful desire and drive, that being able to love and be loved, the young adult pursues the mature love of and intimacy with another. Attachment to a loving and beloved other contains and expresses the love of one's primary experiences. Recapturing the primary love as it has pronounced itself and has so precisely ushered in all subsequent experiences and qualities of love and intimation holds the very meaning of livelihood. Falling in love in adulthood is constituted by both ego progression and ego regression. In fact, falling in love, in its either healthy or misguided sense, necessarily marks this polarity. Progression and ego maturation in all realms of life inherently involve temporary and periodic regressions to earlier states of self-formation. Falling in love is a return to and recapturing of the love with one's primary figure of attachment. The adult's ego upon finding that one special person is exalted, expanded, indeed overly exaggerated. It is one's ego-ideal that is externalized, projected into the partner, and then reinternalized and absorbed by the ego, thereby inflating the ego. This constitutes the ecstasy of mature love, especially in its newness and its promise for the future and confirmation of the past. The subtle pain the adult carries in the ambivalence of having lost one's primary experience of love is both addressed and absolved in the courtship and romance of the great fall into love. The wounded ego is repaired. And the past, so yearned for, is reinstated and affirmed in its foundational success in having molded the present desire and capacity to profess oneself in the acts of mature love, intimacy, and attachment.

Adult love is not, however, merely a re-experiencing of the blissful fusion of the self and the self of the symbiotic mother. Indeed, to love is to form and to express healthy identifications with many close and important persons during the course of childhood and adolescence. In fact, one never ceases to form identifications and through the lifespan utilize these precious identifications as the means of developing and experiencing a loving relationship with another.

The romance of adult love in its maturity involves a blurring of self-boundaries. During coitus, ego boundaries normatively weaken between the two lovers, promoting the ecstatic pleasure of sexual intercourse and orgasm. Subjectively, there is a fusion of persons, a wonderful merger between the

partners of love and desire. This in effect reconstitutes the paralleled symbiotic bliss of the mother-infant attachment and fosters a healthy alliance
between the adult partners. The sense of oneness with a loving and beloved
other is what generates the romanticism and lays the foundation for the maturity of mutual commitment and genuine concern and empathy. Sexual passion
so acutely and sensitively expresses this maturity and ensures its continuity.
Transient and periodic regressions to the primitivism of symbiotic merger
wherein self-other distinction is blurred, both paradoxically and healthily
encourage the appropriate and functional differentiation of adult egos. Again,
the mature love and sexuality of adulthood is in effect both a regressive and
progressive phenomenon. This is the healthy organizational nature of love
and loving attachment.

Mature love and sexual intimacy serve as the bedrock from which a
woman and man concertedly forge their creative union. The couple supports one another's individual development as adults, resultingly unifying
the partnership's effort toward healthily integrative aims and aspirations.
Parenthood is such an aim and desire, yet it is more than a goal. It is in fact
an organizational drive incorporated into the couple's loving attachment.
Their child is the biologically and psychologically expressive link between
the two lovers. As sexuality consummates the mature love between partners,
the planning and actualization of childbearing and childrearing formulate the
very personal and intimate meaning and purpose of their bond. The mutually
articulated creation of a child ushers in the necessity for a new and different
kind of relatedness in which each partner is afforded the opportunity to grow
and mature. The parental partners capitalize on their individual enhancement
to solidify their loving relationship and promulgate their unified efforts as an
adult couple in an adult world.

A parental alliance is formed. The couple mean something more to one
another than just partners of love and intimacy. They have an important task
at hand—to forge an allied partnership geared specifically toward the effective parenting of their child. To the extent that the relationship is healthy
and functional, the partners are likely to effect their parenting with a degree
of competence and assuredness. They not only maintain and build their loving attachment as an intimate couple, they naturally recognize, respect, and
confirm one another's parental duties and the responsibility with which they
assume these duties. This is a reciprocally supportive endeavor, as the necessity of personal esteem and strength comes to weigh on both partners. Being
a parent is a difficult job and this becomes acutely evident.

Every adult who chooses parenthood desires from the heart to be a good
parent. The degree to which one succeeds is clearly quite variable, yet no
adult expressedly chooses to be an ineffective parent. The motive for good

motherhood and fatherhood transcends a mere desire to be competent at whatever one does. Effectively parenting the fruit of one's own being is indeed an ego aspiration, a realization of one's own value and influence as a human being. The good mother and the good father take particular pride in raising a child who, in becoming his or her own person of unique makeup and expression, meets the personal ideal and representation of the parents. This constitutes a profoundly significant execution of the parents' ideals. This is the ultimate of gratification.

Insofar as the parents' ego-ideals are fulfilled by their beloved child and their effective parenting, mother and father succeed in a shared endeavor, the goal of which is not narcissistic gratification or the altruistic desire to offer a gift to one's partner. The child is not designated to complete the parents' unachieved ideals and aspirations. Rather, the child is one for whom to care, and intimate and empathize with for the sake of the child and his or her developing ego aspirations. To the extent that the child secures these endeavors is the extent to which the parents subjectively share in the fulfilling experience. It takes well beyond the sexual act to bear a healthy, happy, well integrated child. It requires more than true love to do the same. Productive love is founded on the functional interdependence of the couple as both lovers and parents.

Parents who hold themselves in personal esteem and confirmation as individuals and as partners in both love and parenthood are sufficiently assured in themselves and their child to clearly differentiate their personal beings. It is inevitable that at least on an unconscious level the boundaries between the loving parent and loving child weaken, allowing their egos to permeate one another. This phenomenon holds potential for the healthy enrichment of identifications on the part of both parties. Parents do in fact project and play out their unresolved past conflicts in interaction with their children. Equally, parents seek in their child the promise of actualization of their aspirations and dreams. It takes psychologically healthy and mature parents as individuals to not exaggerate their real talents and strengths as well as to not be defeated by their own shortcomings as they are illuminated in the parenting process.

It is true that parents do healthily utilize their child, in whom they see themselves in personal reflection, to offer themselves assuredness of maternal and paternal proficiency. The child, to the extent that he or she is secure in his or her budding personhood, offers this functional service with very subtle conscious or unconscious effort. For the parents and the child to meet on common ground of understanding and appreciation, a certain healthy regression on the part of mother and father must occur. This regression is in service to the child as the parents retrieve memories, both of positive and negative valence, of their childhood experiences at their child's current age. Regression to their own childhood also affords the parents the opportunity to check their parenting effectiveness. All of this occurs under the auspices of genuine concern and empathy on the part of the parents for their beloved child in the throes of maturation. Additionally and equally, the parents empathize with themselves as the children of their past in their families of origin. And they empathize with themselves in current adulthood as parents lovingly wishing only to do the best that they can in their parenting endeavors.

The child progressively matures and individuates, relying gradually less on parental support, mirroring, and projection. He or she is capable of selectively internalizing and utilizing those parental urges and pursuits that are in more healthy service to the expanding self, such as concern and sensitivity, empathy and tenderness, nurturance and supportiveness. These loving expressions are at the core of what all parents wish to be. They are representative of what the parents either did or did not experience in their childhood, and therewith are most certainly of what they strive to continually offer their beloved offspring.

Effective parenting is not a static event. The inevitable changes in family life necessitate that parents remain flexible. Their individual personalities as well as their parenting motifs modify in adaptation to and accommodation of the maturation of their child. With each developmental phase of the child's life, the mother and father integrate their perceptions and views of their evolving progeny with those of the child during the previous phase. The continually modifying consideration of their child is, additionally, in constant integration with the image of the fantasied, wished-for child that parents invariably hold on to, at least at an unconscious level. In this regard, parenthood is never a specifically steady activity. As the child's personhood changes in the course of maturation, so, too, do the parents' identities, not only as parenting figures but also as individual beings.

The courses of both parental and childhood transformation are fraught with potential hardship, perhaps especially for the parents. At hand is the parental task of maintaining personal understanding, empathy, support, and nurturance of and for their loved one. There is potential at any juncture of childhood development for the parents to succumb to self-doubt and feelings of inadequacy. Child and parents may become estranged from one another should the parents fail to provide support and confirmation of their child. Effective parents, in face of this potential failing, hold true and firm to their identities, as imperfectly founded as they inevitably are, and offer their identities in parental unification aimed at providing strength, wisdom, and protection for their child. Parents are, after all, the objects of perfection and idealization to their young aspiring offspring. It is imperative that they maintain confidence in themselves both individually and collectively in the service of love and intimacy with an attachment to their beloved child.

Afterword

What is so uniquely splendid about this thing we call love is its inherently elemental nature. Aside from the scientifically founded biological, neurological, and hormonal components that form the genesis of love, there is also the purely human relationship context in which love, intimacy, and attachment form and flourish. What can be more elemental in nature than the psychologically and socially potent bond between a mother and her baby? It is my hope that this book has captured and illuminated the unique, yet universal, phenomenon of primary love, if by no other means than descriptively. Leave it to the wise and learned to exact a definition of love. Leave it to the rest of us, including the mother nestling her progeny securely in her arms, to know love by simply experiencing it.

However simply or complexly, love evolves, transforms, sophisticates, expands, and matures, while securely retaining its primacy. A person's encounters of love through the span of life form a stratum of human experiences, each layer of personal and interpersonal relationship adding to, yet emanating from, all previous ones. Hence, every life event becomes a recreation of something already known, and in the ideal, much revered. Recapturing the harmonious and blissful security of earlier held attachments need not preclude ego advancement, nor need it equate with some form or another of regressive psychopathology. Quite the contrary, that which we lovingly possessed and so fervently wish to renew is precisely that which gives us the impetus and the resourcefulness to uniquely mature, differentiate, and individuate. And with this achievement, we claim for ourselves an integral position in the social world.

The emotion of love is a very natural one. The human being is innately endowed with love's capacity, given a facilitative environment. An environment that promotes love is one that for the child incorporates an effective mother, father, and significant others in an evolving relationship process that is guided and encouraged by these persons. It is our social and cultural organization that at least subtly fosters the appropriate integration of sexuality and love, permitting persons, at the reach of adulthood, to reinforce and vicariously experience and express one another. Sexual love is, in healthy part, a regressive phenomenon in that it takes us back to all previous loves that provide for its self-assuring generativity. A human's prolonged childhood, and all of the sensed goodness of attachment that childhood typically guarantees, leaves us forever yearning for love's continuity and expansion. We adults fervently wish for the genital expression of a true love and the afforded opportunity to pay honor and homage to the earliest loves of our lives. Sexuality without love leaves us in emotional deprivation.

Our prolonged childhood also teaches us that we are dependent beings, undeniably reliant on parental love and admiration. We persistently seek the reassurance of our parents' devotion by vicariously recreating our experiences with them. However, recreating the original and subsequent loves of our lives is not a simple, direct, or guaranteed process. It is riddled with potential pitfalls regardless of our purely and honestly benevolent attempts to secure that which in the past has offered us a sense of personal well-being. Our infantile experiences of primary love have not been, and cannot be, of total, unalloyed perfection. Recreating the mother of goodness is inherently an incomplete pursuit. As noted, no mother is perfect because no human is perfect, and we do not live our lives in a perfect, all-gratifying world. Resultingly, we relentlessly search through life for what has been, with heartfelt despair, deemed missing or denied in our relationships with our parents.

In normality, a healthy and well-integrated adult claims his or her unique identity by means of an integrative identification with the loving and beloved parents while also drawing a clear distinction and differentiation of one's being from the parental beings. Full individuation and autonomy, while a struggle for all persons, is nonetheless the gauge by which the healthy individual relinquishes the appreciated good ties to mother and father, allowing for advancement to the adult level of mature love and sexuality. Only then does love assume the vitality and spirit that makes personhood a truly progressive, rather than an only regressive, movement. With a new love, women and men traverse the path of adulthood as based and expanded on, not trapped in, childhood. In our current relationships with chosen adult lovers, we need not make the frequently futile attempts to correct our past. The ability to accomplish the life tasks of identity formation and independent functioning result in our successes with mature and unconflicted love.

Given the stated fact that life's encounter is not one of perfection and ideality, we inevitably encounter frustrated wishes, parental imperfections, and disappointing attachments. We discover that the processes of love, intimacy, and attachment are not as smooth and successful as described in this book. Yet, when most of us take a hard and honest look at our personal insecurities, inadequacies, shames, humiliations, and desperations, those to which we painfully and regretfully cling, we discover that we in actuality achieve more of the herein presented course of love than we tend to immediately acknowledge. We are thusly healthier than perhaps we think we are. And we have our "imperfect" yet good enough parents to thank for this. If the relationship phenomena described in this book seem too foreign to one's experiences, then one's world can sadly be only of despair and emptiness. In a future volume, I will discuss this human dilemma—that of love's failing.

For those of us fortunate enough to have experienced the finding and re-finding—indeed, the creating and recreating of our love of origin, without undue internal conflicts and trepidation, we humbly and graciously revel in love's offerings. It is of human course that once we encounter the gift of love, we desperately and hopefully cling to it, never wishing to abandon its supremacy.

We love because we have been loved.

Notes

PREFACE

1. Balint, M. (1953). *Primary love and psycho-analytic technique*. New York: Liveright.

INTRODUCTION

1. Balint, M. (1953). *Primary love and psycho-analytic technique*. New York: Liveright.

CHAPTER 1

1. Giovacchini, P.L. (1972). The symbiotic phase. In P.L. Giovacchini (Ed.), *Tactics and techniques in psychoanalytic therapy* (pp. 137–169). New York: Science House.

2. Sandler, J. and Sandler, A.M. (1978). On the development of object relationships and affects. *International Journal of Psychoanalysis*, 59, 285–296.

3. Blank, G. and Blank, R. (1979). *Ego psychology II: Psychoanalytic developmental psychology*. New York: Columbia University Press.

4. Blatt, S. (1974). Levels of object representation in anaclitic and introjective depression. *Psychoanalytic Study of the Child*, 29, 107–157.

5. Burgner, M. and Edgcumbe, R. (1972). Some problems in the conceptualization of early object relationships: The concept of object constancy. *Psychoanalytic Study of the Child*, 27, 315–333.

6. Dare, C. and Holder, A. (1981). Developmental aspects of the interaction between narcissism, self-esteem, and object relations. *International Journal of Psychoanalysis*, 62, 323–337.

7. Lichtenberg, J. (1981). Implications for psychoanalytic theory of research on the neonate. *International Review of Psychoanalysis*, 8, 35–52.

8. Meissner, W.W. (1986). The earliest internalizations. In R. Lax, S. Bach, and J.A. Burland (Eds.), *Self and object constancy* (pp. 29–72). New York: Guilford Press.

9. Balint, M. (1953). *Primary love and psycho-analytic technique.* New York: Liveright.

10. Neubauer, P. (1985). Preoedipal objects and object primacy. *Psychoanalytic Study of the Child*, 40, 163–182.

11. Noy, P. (1984). The three components of empathy. In J. Lichtenberg, M. Bornstein, and D. Silver (Eds.), *Empathy I.* (pp. 167–199). Hillsdale, NJ.: Analytic Press.

CHAPTER 2

1. Bowlby, J. (1969). *Attachment and loss: Vol 1. Attachment.* New York: Basic Books.

2. Blum, H. (1977). Masochism, the ego ideal, and the psychology of women. In H. Blum (Ed.), *Female psychology: Contemporary psychoanalytic views* (pp. 157–191). New York: International Universities Press.

3. Chodorow, N. (1978). *The reproduction of mothering: Psychoanalysis and the sociology of gender.* Berkeley, CA.: University of California Press.

4. Jessner, L., Weigert, E., and Foy, J. (1970). The development of parental attitudes during pregnancy. In E.J. Anthony and T. Benedek (Eds.), *Parenthood: Its psychology and psychopathology* (pp. 209–244). Boston: Little, Brown and Company.

5. Anthony, E.J. (1984). Creative parenthood. In R. Cohen, B. Cohler, and S. Weissman (Eds.), *Parenthood: A psychodynamic perspective* (pp. 24–32). New York: Guilford.

6. Benedek, T. (1970). Motherhood and nurturing. In E.J. Anthony and T. Benedek (Eds.), *Parenthood: Its psychology and psychopathology* (pp. 153–165). Boston: Little, Brown and Company.

7. Deutsch, H. (1945). *The psychology of women: A psychoanalytic interpretation: Vol 2. Motherhood.* New York: Grune and Stratton.

CHAPTER 3

1. Kohut, H. (1971). *The analysis of the self.* New York: International Universities Press.

2. Winnicott, D.W. (1955). The depressive position in normal emotional development. *British Journal of Medical Psychology*, 28, 89–100.

3. Benedek, T. (1970). Motherhood and nurturing. In E.J. Anthony and T. Benedek (Eds.), *Parenthood: Its psychology and psychopathology* (pp. 153–165). Boston: Little, Brown and Company.

4. Sandler, J. and Sandler, A.M. (1978). On the development of object relationships and affects. *International Journal of Psychoanalysis*, 59, 285–296.

5. Benedek, T. (1959). Parenthood as a developmental phase: A contribution to the libido theory. *Journal of the American Psychoanalytic Association*, 7, 389–417.

6. Winnicott, D.W. (1965). *The maturational processes and the facilitating environment: Studies in the theory of emotional development.* New York: International Universities Press.

7. Lichtenberg, J. (1975). The development of the sense of self. *Journal of the American Psychoanalytic Association*, 23, 453–483.

8. Brazelton, T.B. (1979). Four early stages in the development of mother-infant interaction. *Psychoanalytic Study of the Child*, 34, 349–369.

9. Winnicott, D.W. (1971). *Playing and reality.* New York: Basic Books.

10. Spitz, R. (1965). *The first year of life: A psychoanalytic study of normal and deviant development of object relations.* New York: International Universities Press.

11. Lichtenberg, J. (1975). The development of the sense of self. *Journal of the American Psychoanalytic Association*, 23, 453–483.

CHAPTER 4

1. Benedek, T. (1959). Parenthood as a developmental phase: A contribution to the libido theory. *Journal of the American Psychoanalytic Association*, 7, 389–417.

2. Elson, M. (1984). Parenthood and the transformations of narcissism. In R. Cohen, B. Cohler, and S. Weissman (Eds.), *Parenthood: A psychodynamic perspective* (pp. 297–314). New York: Guilford.

3. Ross, J.M. (1977). Towards fatherhood: The epigenesis of paternal identity during a boy's first decade. *International Review of Psychoanalysis*, 4, 327–347.

4. Burlingham, D. (1973). The preoedipal infant-father relationship. *Psychoanalytic Study of the Child*, 25, 23–47.

5. Ross, J.M. (1975). The development of paternal identity: A critical review of the literature on nurturance and generativity in boys and men. *Journal of the American Psychoanalytic Association*, 23, 783–817.

6. Cohen, R. and Weissman, S. (1984). The parenting alliance. In R. Cohen, B. Cohler, and S. Weissman (Eds.), *Parenthood: A psychodynamic perspective* (pp. 33–49). New York: Guilford.

7. Gurwitt, A. (1976). Aspects of prospective fatherhood: A case report. *Psychoanalytic Study of the Child*, 31, 237–271.

8. Sadow, L. (1984). The psychological origins of parenthood. In R. Cohen, B. Cohler, and S. Weissman (Eds.), *Parenthood: A psychodynamic perspective* (pp. 285–296). New York: Guilford.

9. Ross, J.M. (1984). Fathers in development: An overview of recent contributions. In R. Cohen, B. Cohler, and S. Weissman (Eds.), *Parenthood: A psychodynamic perspective* (373–390). New York: Guilford.

10. Atkins, R. (1981). Finding one's father: The mother's contribution to early father representations. *Journal of the American Academy of Psychoanalysis*, 9, 539–559.

CHAPTER 5

1. Spitz, R. (1965). *The first year of life: A psychoanalytic study of normal and deviant development of object relations*. New York: International Universities Press.

2. Mahler, M., Pine, F. and Bergman, A. (1975). *The psychological birth of the human infant: Symbiosis and individuation*. New York: Basic Books.

3. Bergman, A. (1980). Ours, yours, mine. In R. Lax, S. Bach, and J.A. Burland (Eds.), *Rapprochement: The critical subphase of separation-individuation* (pp. 199–216). Northvale, NJ.: Jason Aronson.

4. Winnicott, D.W. (1971). *Playing and reality*. New York: Basic Books.

5. Bergman, A. (1980). Ours, yours, mine. In R. Lax, S. Bach, and J.A. Burland (Eds.), *Rapprochement: The critical subphase of separation-individuation* (pp. 199–216). Northvale, NJ.: Jason Aronson.

6. McDevitt, J. (1980). The role of internalization in the development of object relations during the separation-individuation phase. In R. Lax, S. Bach, and J.A. Burland (Eds.), *Rapprochement: The critical subphase of separation-individuation.* (pp.135–149). Northvale, NJ.: Jason Aronson.

7. Joffe, W.G. and Sandler, J. (1965). Notes on pain, depression, and individuation. *Psychoanalytic Study of the Child*, 20, 394–424.

8. Pine, F. (1989). The place of object loss in normal development. In D. Dietrich and P. Shabad (Eds.), *The problem of loss and mourning: Psychoanalytic perspectives* (pp. 159–173). New York: International Universities Press.

9. Lichtenberg, J. (1975). The development of the sense of self. *Journal of the American Psychoanalytic Association*, 23, 453–484.

CHAPTER 6

1. Piaget, J. (1952). *The origins of intelligence in children*. New York: International Universities Press.

2. Abelin, E. (1971). The role of the father in the separation-individuation process. In J. McDevitt and C. Settlage (Eds.), *Separation-individuation: Essays in honor of Margaret S. Mahler* (pp. 229–252). New York: International Universities Press.

3. Scharff, D. and Scharff, J.S. (1987). *Object relations family therapy*. Northvale, N.J.: Jason Aronson.

4. Jacobson, E. (1964). *The self and the object world.* New York: International Universities Press.

5. Tyson, P. (1982). A developmental line of gender identity, gender role, and choice of love object. *Journal of the American Psychoanalytic Association,* 30, 61–86.

6. Chodorow, N. (1978). *The reproduction of mothering:Psychoanalysis and the sociology of gender.* Berkeley, CA.: University of California Press.

7. Ibid.

8. Tyson, P. (1982). A developmental line of gender identity, gender role, and choice of love object. *Journal of the American Psychoanalytic Association,* 30, 61–86.

CHAPTER 7

1. Scharff, D. and Scharff, J.S. (1987). *Object relations family therapy.* Northvale, NJ.: Jason Aronson.

2. Blos, P. (1962). *On adolescence: A psychoanalytic interpretation.* New York: Free Press.

3. Deutsch, H. (1944). *The psychology of women: A psychoanalytic interpretation, Vol. 1.* New York: Grune and Stratton.

4. Wolf, E. (1982). Adolescence: Psychology of the self and selfobjects. In S. Feinstein, J. Looney, A. Schwartzberg, and A. Sorosky (Eds.), *Adolescent psychiatry: Developmental and clinical studies, vol. 10* (pp. 171–181). Chicago: University of Chicago Press.

5. Freud, A. (1958). Adolescence. *Psychoanalytic Study of the Child,* 13, 255–278.

6. Deutsch, H. (1967). *Selected problems of adolescence: With special emphasis on group formation.* New York: International Universities Press.

7. Laufer, M. (1964). Ego ideal and pseudo ego ideal in adolescence. *Psychoanalytic Study of the Child,* 19, 196–221.

8. Jacobson, E. (1964). *The self and the object world.* New York: International Universities Press.

9. Greenacre, P. (1975). Differences between male and female adolescent sexual development as seen from longitudinal studies. In S. Feinstein and P. Giovacchini (Eds.), *Adolescent psychiatry: Developmental and clinical studies, vol. 4,* (pp. 105–120). Northvale, NJ.: Jason Aronson.

10. Erikson, E. (1956). The problem of ego identity. *Journal of the American Psychoanalytic Association,* 4, 56–121.

11. Weissman, S. and Barglow, P. (1980). Recent contributions to the theory of female adolescent psychological development. In S. Feinstein, P. Giovacchini, J. Looney, A. Schwartzberg, and A. Sorosky (Eds.), *Adolescent psychiatry: Developmental and clinical studies, vol. 8* (pp. 214–230). Chicago: University of Chicago Press.

12. Greenacre, P. (1975). Differences between male and female adolescent sexual development as seen from longitudinal studies. In S. Feinstein and P. Giovacchini (Eds.), *Adolescent psychiatry: Developmental and clinical studies, vol. 4*, (pp. 105–120). Northvale, NJ.: Jason Aronson.

13. Chodorow, N. (1978). *The reproduction of mothering: Psychoanalysis and the sociology of gender*. Berkeley, CA.: University of California Press.

14. Geleerd, E. (1961). Some aspects of ego vicissitudes in adolescence. *Journal of the American Psychoanalytic Association*, 9, 394–405.

15. Moore, W.T. (1975). Some economic functions of genital masturbation during adolescent development. In I. Marcus and J. Francis (Eds.), *Masturbation: From infancy to senescence* (pp. 231–276). New York: International Universities Press.

16. Wolf, E. (1982). Adolescence: Psychology of the self and selfobjects. In S. Feinstein, J. Looney, A. Schwartzberg, and A. Sorosky (Eds.), *Adolescent psychiatry: Developmental and clinical studies, vol. 10* (pp. 171–181). Chicago: University of Chicago Press.

17. Laufer, M. and Laufer, M.E. (1984). *Adolescence and developmental breakdown: A psychoanalytic view*. New Haven, CT.: Yale University Press.

18. Erikson, E. (1959). *Identity and the life cycle*. New York: International Universities Press.

CHAPTER 8

1. Bergmann, M. (1988). Freud's three theories of love in the light of later developments. *Journal of the American Psychoanalytic Association*, 36, 653–672.

2. Ibid.

3. Bak, R. (1973). Being in love and object loss. *International Journal of Psychoanalysis*, 54, 1–8.

4. Chasseguet-Smirgel, J. (1976). Some thoughts on the ego ideal: A contribution to the study of the 'illness of ideality.' *Psychoanalytic Quarterly*, 45, 345–373.

5. Kremen, H. and Kremen, B. (1971). Romantic love and idealization. *American Journal of Psychoanalysis*, 31, 134–143.

6. Kernberg, O. (1980). Love, the couple, and the group: A psychoanalytic frame. *Psychoanalytic Quarterly*, 49, 78–108.

7. Kernberg, O. (1974). Mature love: Prerequisites and characteristics. *Journal of the American Psychoanalytic Association*, 22, 743–768.

8. Bollas, C. (1984–85). Loving hate. *The Annual of Psychoanalysis*, 12–13, 221–237.

9. Binstock, W. (1973). On the two forms of intimacy. *Journal of the American Psychoanalytic Association*, 21, 93–107.

10. Klein, R. (1990). *Object relations and the family process*. New York: Praeger.

11. Bergmann, M. (1971). Psychoanalytic observations on the capacity to love. In J. McDevitt and C. Settlage (Eds.), *Separation-individuation: Essays in honor of Margaret S. Mahler* (pp. 15–40). New York: International Universities Press.

12. Bergmann, M. (1980). On the intrapsychic function of falling in love. *Psychoanalytic Quarterly*, 49, 56–77.

13. Bergmann, M. (1971). Psychoanalytic observations on the capacity to love. In J. McDevitt and C. Settlage (Eds.), *Separation-individuation: Essays in honor of Margaret S. Mahler* (pp. 15–40). New York: International Universities Press.

14. Bak, R. (1973). Being in love and object loss. *International Journal of Psychoanalysis*, 54, 1–8.

CHAPTER 9

1. Klein, R. (1990). *Object relations and the family process*. New York: Praeger.

2. Willi, J. (1982). *Couples in collusion: The unconscious dimension in partner relationships*. Claremont, CA.: Hunter House.

3. Kernberg, O. (1974). Mature love: Prerequisites and characteristics. *Journal of the American Psychoanalytic Association*, 22, 743–768.

4. Bergmann, M. (1980). On the intrapsychic function of falling in love. *Psychoanalytic Quarterly*, 49, 56–77.

5. Binstock, W. (1973). On the two forms of intimacy. *Journal of the American Psychoanalytic Association*, 21, 93–107.

6. Kernberg, O. (1977). Boundaries and structure in love relations. *Journal of the American Psychoanalytic Association*, 25, 81–114.

7. Benedek, T. (1977). Ambivalence, passion, and love. *Journal of the American Psychoanalytic Association*, 25, 53–79.

8. Gediman, H. (1975). Reflections on romanticism, narcissism, and creativity. *Journal of the American Psychoanalytic Association*, 23, 407–423.

9. Benedek, T. (1977). Ambivalence, passion, and love. *Journal of the American Psychoanalytic Association*, 25, 53–79.

CHAPTER 10

1. Freud, S. (1917). Mourning and melancholia. *Standard Edition*, 14, 243–258. London: Hogarth Press, 1957.

2. Loewald, H. (1962). Internalization, separation, mourning, and the superego. *Psychoanalytic Quarterly*, 31, 483–504.

3. Joffe, W. and Sandler, J. (1965). Notes on pain, depression, and individuation. *Psychoanalytic Study of the Child*, 20, 394–424.

4. Bowlby, J. (1961). Processes of mourning. *International Journal of Psychoanalysis*, 42, 317–340.

5. Ibid.

6. Ibid.

7. Lipson, C. (1963). Denial and mourning. *International Journal of Psychoanalysis*, 44, 104–107.

8. Wetmore, R. (1967). The role of grief in psychoanalysis. *International Journal of Psychoanalysis*, 48, 97–103.

9. Volkan, V. (1981). *Linking objects and linking phenomena: A study of the forms, symptoms, metapsychology, and therapy of complicated mourning.* New York: International Universities Press.

10. Siggins, L. (1966). Mourning: A critical survey of the literature. *International Journal of Psychoanalysis*, 47, 14–25.

11. Krupp, G. (1965). Identification as a defence against anxiety in coping with loss. *International Journal of Psychoanalysis*, 46, 303–314.

12. Pollack, G. (1961). Mourning and adaptation. *International Journal of Psychoanalysis*, 42, 341–361.